Eusebism

Eusebism

A New Moral Theory

Carlo Prisco

LEXINGTON BOOKS
Lanham • Boulder • New York • London

Published by Lexington Books
An imprint of The Rowman & Littlefield Publishing Group, Inc.
4501 Forbes Boulevard, Suite 200, Lanham, Maryland 20706
www.rowman.com

86-90 Paul Street, London EC2A 4NE, United Kingdom

British Library Cataloguing in Publication Information Available

Library of Congress Cataloging-in-Publication Data

Names: Prisco, Carlo, author.
Title: Eusebism : a new moral theory / Carlo Prisco.
Other titles: Eusebismo morale e diritto. English
Description: Lanham : Lexington Books, 2021. | Includes bibliographical references and index. | Summary: "Based on existing moral philosophy, Carlo Prisco introduces Eusebism as a way to develop new perspectives on being and relating by offering practical tools to approach everyday life and transfer good thought into action" —Provided by publisher.
Identifiers: LCCN 2021036803 (print) | LCCN 2021036804 (ebook) | ISBN 9781666902921 (cloth) | ISBN 9781666902938 (epub)
Subjects: LCSH: Ethics. | Respect. | Law—Philosophy.
Classification: LCC BJ1134 .P7513 2021 (print) | LCC BJ1134 (ebook) | DDC 171/.2—dc23
LC record available at https://lccn.loc.gov/2021036803
LC ebook record available at https://lccn.loc.gov/2021036804

Contents

Introduction

New ideas require new words: from this consideration arose the need to look for a word that could encompass many different instances.

Using terms that create division, we have ended up drawing dividing lines between groups that do not even exist, or would not exist, without our need to separate and make distinctions.

An animal rights advocate, for example, in name or fact, is limited to something very specific that is considered predominant and absorbing.

We could say the same about a pacifist, as well as an environmentalist or a human rights advocate: all of them will have far more stratified and profound ideas than what the conceptual framework underlying the definitions allows to transpire, yet what "filters out" is only that flag, which ends up absorbing (and thus overwhelming) everything else.

General classifications of thought concerning individual aspects of the person cannot define someone's ideas.

The psychological phenomenon is quite well known and has been amply demonstrated with the famous Stanford[1] "prison experiment," which could be summarized as follows: if you take any person, put on a hat, give him a flag and a social role, that person will act exactly like the hat, flag, and society presuppose.

Continuing to feed stereotypes such as the ideological contrast between those who decide to engage in the protection of humans, the environment, nonhumans, and so on means feeding a vicious circle. This implies isolation and inability to identify in the members of distinct "factions," while on the other hand increasing the inherent conflict between those who consider themselves "different."

Frequently, people are animated by the same ideals, simply transposed to different levels, thanks to those mind compartments that prevent them from awareness.

How could you fight for the weak while ignoring nonhuman animals? How can people claim the right to health without engaging in environmental issues, which are the basis of survival for the human species?

At the same time, how can it happen that those who preach respect for plant species do not act for individual animals?

Sometimes the limit is innate. It is also induced by society, which loves labels to flatten and reduce everyone to misleading words.

While I was reading different theories about animals, the environment, human rights, and such, I realized that they were all missing something and were definitely too limited: why not develop a new moral that can be useful in all aspects of life?

My approach to life is that of ancient Greek philosophers: How could you determine good and evil, failing to realize who you are, where do you come from, and what is the real nature of things around you?

Do not judge me because I had the presumption to invent a universal moral theory, daring to give answers valid in any situation of life, everywhere, anytime.

While others suggest you take baby steps, I suggest making a jump, leaving behind unawareness, and embracing awareness.

Thinking about the lowest common denominator, I found that it can only respect: if your life is based on respect, you can reach the stars.

In ancient Greece, the term εὐσέβεια was coined to define a sense of respect of exceptional breadth, as evidenced by the two words that compose it, namely "ευ" (good, good) and "σέβομαι" (respect, venerate).[2]

In the archaic meaning, the term designated the broadest feeling of respect in relationships with others, not just humans.

Acting according to *eusebeia* meant respecting duties, other life forms, and divinities; this word was also used to indicate the concept of dharma in the Greek translation of the Edicts of 250 BC of the Indian emperor Ashoka: conduct such as good faith, moderation, respect for all forms of life, generosity, and compassion can be ascribed to both definitions.

Throughout history, the term *eusebeia* was increasingly identified with religion, both in pagan and Christian cults, losing most of the nuances of the original meaning, which contained within itself the whole precept of living harmoniously and respectfully.

With Eusebism, I wanted to create a thought that places unconditional respect for anything at its foundation.

The visual representation of this thought is the wheel of Eusebism, which symbolizes everything and expresses the universal and innate characteristics that unite everything: the infinitely small and the infinitely large, the visible as the invisible.

At the center is the One, the principle that philosophers like Empedocles already identified millennia ago in the origin of the cosmos, that unity from which everything comes and to which everything returns: the disintegration, symbolized by the rays that radiate from the center, leads to the apparent division, for which each entity believes itself to be distinct from the others, but continues to belong to the same system, represented by the circumference.

The symbol of Eusebism can be interpreted both from a material and a transcendental point of view: in both cases, our origins—whoever or whatever we are—are the same, and we all belong and participate in the same system. At the same time, individuality (or its perception) is limited to a single phase of existence.[3]

Eusebism is something different from everything else but is meant to embrace anything: starting from a *pars destruens* (destructive part, ed.), aimed at identifying and overcoming the conceptual limits and intellectual segregations imposed during so much history of humanity, and culminating in *pars costruens* (building part, ed.), intended to propose new ideas.

I have tried to limit the critical part to essential, while my final goal is to describe something new and original.

You can consider this book as a trip and chapters as stops.

At the end of the trip, we should be able to think and act differently. If you will not, please do not ask for refunds or returns.

First stop: we will analyze many ideas meant to develop new rights or new categories of rightsholders to determine the pros and cons.

Second stop: we will analyze the founding principles of Eusebism.

Third stop: we will focus on the definition and nature of rights.

Fourth stop: applying the principles mentioned above, we will finally build a moral system, determining just or unjust.

Final stop: we will do some practice with our new moral to see how it can help us in everyday life.

I ask you to approach this reading without prejudices: I know that this is virtually impossible because our interpretation of things is always based on experiences and prejudices. Then, just keep your mind open to any possibility.

We need to develop our knowledge on fundamental aspects of life, and awareness will come.

Awareness is also the basis of freedom of choice, especially in a world where actions and their effects are so divided. Pushing a button to launch a missile is completely different from pulling the trigger while looking into a person's eye, just as eating a steak is different from killing the animal.

If it is true that the truth sets you free, then, before making any decision, you should get as much information as possible.

We should also note that reality is made up of information (objective) and interpretation (subjective): we need to separate things to avoid confusion. For example, if someone were to say: *Tom scolded Jack* in the presence of three listeners, one might think that Jack was wrong, thus deserving the scolding of Tom; another might think that Tom was wrong in scolding Jack; the third listener could suspend their judgment until more details were given. In the process of representing reality by everyone, the habits, experiences, aspirations, etc. are involved: the first listener, who considered Tom as a victim of Jack, could be a parent used to scolding their children, while the second could be a young man who still lives with his parents and is used to being scolded frequently. The third listener adopted the best way of thinking, spontaneously suspending judgment without precluding any possibility of understanding.

This is what I am asking you during your reading.

Now, you can fasten your seatbelts and enjoy the ride.

NOTES

1. Lovaglia, Michael J., *Knowing People: The Personal Use Of Social Psychology*, Rowman & Littlefield, 2006, p. 320. In 1973, the psychologist Philip J. Zimbardo, a professor at Stanford University, selected some students to carry out an experiment, also known as the "Stanford prison experiment." The group of students selected to take part in the simulation was randomly divided into two opposing sides: that of the prison guards and that of the prisoners. The two groups began to interact in an environment reproducing a prison, where the guards had discretion about maintaining order. After only five days, the experiment was suspended due to the serious decline of events, as the guards had begun to treat the detainees with humiliating, harassing, and sadistic methods, with significant psychological repercussions on the latter and on their perception of reality.
2. Malherbe Abraham J., Holladay Carl R., Fitzgerald John T., Sterling Gregory E., Thompson James W., *Light From The Gentiles*, Brill Academic Pub, 2013, p. 446.
3. From a strictly physical profile, the original unit is identified with the Big Bang, that is, the initial explosion from which the visible universe derived. The same phenomenon is observed in the subsequent stages, with the formation of stars and planets, which, in turn, through the transformation and distinction of their own elements, give rise to further elements, including the human being.

Chapter 1

Prejudices and Preconceptions

There is no thought without somebody expressing it. There can be no thought without a thinker. The thinkers we know are all human. Each human has different experiences, aspirations, knowledge, character, motivations, interests, feelings, emotions, and perceptions.

There are facts and interpretations: anybody who tells a story also interprets it from his or her perspective. Should many listen to the same story, each of them will focus on different aspects. If requested, in turn, to repeat the story, they will provide different interpretations.

All of us bring an "experience" and have some "strongholds," which are fixed points that we do not consider possible to question, and that guide our evaluations, forecasts, and interpretations.

Euripides invited us to question everything,[1] and this is what a free thinker must do if hoping to get closer to knowledge: this means, in the first place, to strip ourselves of prejudices. On the other hand, we are so wrapped up in everyday life, in our habits and experiences, that we don't even ask ourselves if some things are facts or just the interpretation we have given to them.

Some of the limits to our views derive from objective limitations (i.e., sensory). In contrast, we impose ourselves on others (e.g., identifying categories and considering ourselves included in them). In both cases, we encounter many difficulties in being objective with our views and admitting, or even simply understanding, that they are not.

1.1 A QUESTION OF PERSPECTIVE

The Senses and the Perception of Reality: What if the Sky Wasn't Blue?

Our mind is tuned to definitions like "objective" and "subjective" to distinguish what is "as it really is" from what it is as defined by the observer.

We are also used to consider the reality surrounding us as objective and opinions and ideas as subjective: for example, we consider objective that "the sky is blue" and subjective that "the sky is beautiful." In doing this, we demonstrate our fundamental limitation: we are not aware of our limits.

It is known to all that the human being is limited, but it is not simple to determine his actual bounds. Therefore, we rely on conventions, although we often forget them and confuse them with absolute and objective data.

The perception of what we call "world," or "universe," is limited and subjective: our "visible reality" is only a facet of everything that exists and, to be precise, it is the portion of electromagnetic radiation with a frequency between 400 and 780 THz and between 380 and 780 nm of wavelength.[2]

For example, many insects' vision allows them to see ultraviolet rays and, accordingly, a potentilla flower can reveal only to them the guidelines toward the precious nourishment. In contrast, such lines seem nonexistent to the human observer, as they are imperceptible.[3]

In short, the sky is not necessarily blue, even if we perceive it that way. Not to mention that even what is perceived as "sky" is based on a convention.

Today we can distinguish those lines through technology. Still, we can only probe that part of the Universe (otherwise not visible to the naked eye) our current technology can reveal. Today, as in the time of Socrates, it is, therefore, necessary to remember the precept: "I know that I don't know."

Beyond the conventions about the name of colors, our sensory limitations preclude us from perceiving a large part of what exists around us.

An ambitious project that has recently been developed allows us to observe a part of this "invisible universe": the ALMA radio telescope in Chile is made up of sixty-six antennas (only twenty of which are in operation) that can detect wavelengths about a thousand times greater than that of visible light and function as a single, huge instrument.[4]

The human perspective is based on partial elements and extremely limited knowledge of the main phenomena of the surrounding world and, since that knowledge is extremely fallacious, it is necessary to seek a way that could help us going through these limitations.

When speaking of the limits of human perceptions, we often tend to trust them, sure that only (one) god has got absolute and impartial knowledge.

The objection could be correct, but it is misleading: we do not need to ignore human limits to overcome their side effects, but it is enough to recognize them to know their results and, therefore, comprehend what is relative from what is absolute.

For example, stating with certainty that nothing exists that is not visible to the human eye represents a prejudice based on the relativity of our perceptions. To overcome it, it is unnecessary to know what exists beyond the visible: it is enough to know that something more may exist since we have sensory limitations.

At this point, even without aspiring to divine skills, each of us can escape the trap of absolute categorizations based on those prejudices we ignored.

Redefine Thinking

One of the main problems of philosophy, especially modern philosophy, is having completely lost sight of the essential issues and having confused the formulation of thought with the study of others' ideas.

Adopting a critical perspective toward other thinkers is different from inventing new thoughts. The schematism of thought into which one ends up falling creates contrapositions based on specious lucubration.

The "currents of thought" arise from the historical-critical method to which modern philosophers claim to belong or which they criticize, confusing the history of philosophy with philosophy itself.

The development of critical sense and the learning of philosophical topics and methods do not represent an absolute value but only a tool to help the understanding of reality and existence.

It is not mandatory to go along with somebody else's thought just because it was a new philosophical invention in the past nor to explain if that thought is right or wrong and why. The contribution of free thinkers is to reveal what is useful, while the evaluation and a possible comparison between their thoughts are others' matter.

In the ancient world, social contexts were culturally homogeneous: since there was no means of mass communication, and traveling was very rare and limited, everybody was affected by a few influences, but decisive, because they were free of contradictions.

Today the cultural influences, at least in the Western world, are even too many: each of us suffers from daily overstimulation of aspirations[5] and a constant bombardment of ideas, suggestions, opinions, criticisms, requests, invitations, and such.

On the one hand, a greater number of ideas lead to more comparisons between them and, therefore, a lower probability of prejudice than a culturally "closed" world; on the other hand, there are nowadays a greater number of prejudices to beware of.

Western society is undergoing a massive process of homologation, owing to television and the internet. Still, cultural globalization does not go hand in hand with this phenomenon. On the contrary, a division by macro-areas occurs (or continues) based on the sharing of linguistic families, religious beliefs, geographical location, and ethnicity.

In Western societies, the consumerist model is the main one, and the over-stimulation of the aspirations above promotes it. Everybody should aspire to something more than what they already own to spend money to buy goods or services sold by others.

Advertisements are omnipresent and are the foundation of the consumerist system. It is not a coincidence that the expression "*advertising is the soul of commerce*" is the key slogan.

The real issue is that advertising creates demand where there is not, and it has evolved to convince customers that they need something they never even knew they wanted.

The difference between an informative advertisement and a persuasive advertisement is that the former simply says, "I exist, and I do this in this way." The latter can omit all of the above and simply convey the message "you want it/you need it."

Unfortunately, the cultural contamination of advertising has reached levels that characterize the thinking of most members of society at all levels: from the prevalence of material over the spiritual, from the relationship with one-self and with one's fellow man, to that with animals and the environment.

Of course, it is not only advertising that influences the "collective feeling" or way of thinking, since television broadcasts continue to play a decisive role in this: the selection of information and the ways to spread it already represents an instrument of influence and interference with the free will of each person.

The terms used, the topics discussed, the way famous people or those who appear on television dress or have their hair done have a reflection in all viewers: for this reason, in the United States, for example, it is considered unanimously improper and even a crime to show naked scenes on television, while in Europe this is widely accepted.

We can legitimately exclude that all people born in the United States have a particular inner or genetic predisposition for considering nudity obscene. Therefore, we must conclude that the same people, born or living in Europe, would consider it normal.

Social influence is a well-known phenomenon, but what is often not considered is how much each one runs the risk of acting out for social emulation rather than out of conviction.

Before becoming free thinkers, we must deal with being members of a family, a local community, a nation, an area of the world, and, finally, of the world itself.

Social transformations are much slower than individual transformations since each tends to perpetuate their suggestions and habits, or, at least, to deal with them.

To free ourselves from suggestions, we must resort to a process of objectification of reality, which can begin in this way: let us ask ourselves if what we do is the result of our choices or if we have been induced to act by emulation.

For example: did I choose the footwear I wear because, if I had to imagine one type of shoe, would I have chosen it this way? Did I choose among the alternatives that others have proposed to me? Or have I chosen from alternatives prepared by somebody based on the fashion?

If we were free and emancipated, there would be no reason why all Westerners wear suits with shirts and ties on solemn occasions, instead of, for example, togas or tunics worn by our ancestors (or still in use by many populations of the world), which are more comfortable and much cheaper.

Thanks to objectification, we can determine what we think and prefer, transforming ourselves from simple emulators or decision-makers into real creators.

1.2 ANTHROPOCENTRISM AND HUMANISM

The history of thought or, if you prefer, of philosophy is similar to that of our everyday life, and that leads us to see what we want to see and describes it as it is. But on the other hand, even philosophers tend to certain habits endowed with sensitivity, specific interests, and such.

It is certainly not a coincidence that the prevailing current of thought in the human world is the anthropocentric one; in fact, we will see that it is much easier to formulate thoughts that advantage us than contradict us.

Understanding this phenomenon will help to identify the main limits deriving from prejudice, handed down to us at a cultural level, which prevents us from considering the interests of those we place outside the human community.

Anthropocentrism means placing man (ο άνθρωπός) at the center of the world and describes a phenomenon that has different implications. For example, it can be a sense-made philosophical thought, a psychological attitude, or even a simple behavior.

You can think or act anthropocentrically or do both.

The basic idea is that human beings dominate over everything else that they can freely use: from this perspective, all human beings are considered indiscriminately, regardless of specificities such as gender, ethnicity, and such.

Those who embrace this conception believe that humans rise beyond any form of animal life. Thus, for example, when Darwin formulated his evolutionist theory, many people manifested their anthropocentrism by accusing it of heresy and mocking the possibility that we had evolved from apes.

Of course, there is no unity of thought in the field of anthropocentrism. Therefore, we can include numerous nuances, from the most fundamentalist ones, which still reject evolutionism, to the more open ones, which consider the predominance of man both as a source of rights and duties: a bit like a good father, in short, he can use his power on his children, but must protect them at the same time.

Any anthropocentric perspective considers human beings as the judges of the fate of everything around them on a conscious or unconscious level.

Anthropocentric culture dominates the Western world today, but this has not always been this way.

The Orphic doctrine[6] was born in ancient Greece, which considered human beings as formed by a subtle and pure component, the soul, and by a heavy and imperfect body: this central perspective focused on the theory of soul reincarnation as an instrument to better get back to the unity of origin.[7]

The Orphics also attributed spiritual qualities to anything that transcends the human being and belongs to kingdoms other than the animal one.

The Greek world, characterized by paganism and largely influenced by Orphic cults, had continued to consider humankind coexistent with animals, where the former has its order based on customary laws and the latter based on their law of nature.

Protagoras' (486 BC–411 BC) philosophical thought conceived things only concerning human beings value, recognizable in the definition that Plato attributes to him: "I, for me, sustain that the truth is as I wrote: each of us is the measure of things that are and are not."[8] This statement generally coincides with the origin of humanist thought, which places the human being at the center of all things.

Eternal Rome

Roman culture, which flourished between the eighth century BC and the fifth century AD, represented, in many ways, the negation of Greek culture, or at least of the Athenian culture that was born in a city and then permeated not only the area but many of the places and kingdoms reached by colonization, conquest, or trade.

The quintessential legacy of ancient Greece to the world is philosophy, the sublimation of the intellect, arts, and literature. On the other hand, Rome was based on completely different assumptions and dominated by an interest in what is material: physical strength, military organization, monumental architecture, violent spectacles, admiration for military triumphs, as well as political and economic successes.

To satisfy the taste of the macabre and unusual, the Romans brought about the first extinctions of entire animal species, deporting them from the colonies to the Eternal City. This was made to sacrifice them in rituals and perverse circus games, which were more prestigious when more heterogeneous were the animal species.

Hot baths represented for ancient Rome something more than a simple place for recreation or relaxation: they were a social place for meeting and attending society and a regular health habit.[9]

The Roman model, the main example of globalization, was exported to all conquered regions and adopted by new cities. Every new and important city had its hot baths and theaters.

The heating of water rooms at the baths and in the houses was made possible by the combustion of wood, also widely used to build war fleets. For this reason, we can date back to Roman times, the first animal extinctions, and the first large-scale deforestation caused by man.[10]

The contemporary Western mentality represents the evolution of the Roman one: beyond the proclaims and lone voices, we perpetuate the stereotype of military power, strength as a means for peace, of the dominance of the strong over the weak, of the winner over the defeated, and such.

Like Sparta, the Roman cultural ideal establishes the equivalence between possibility and right: *if* I can conquer a country, *then* I have the right to do so.

It is not a question of written laws but of a mental and psychological approach proper to the evolution of society, which develops an economic, administrative, bureaucratic, and military system that has a few comparisons elsewhere.

After the collapse of the Roman Empire and the affirmation of Christianity, the social model has changed considerably. But mental habits are almost unchanged and have come to us through a journey that lasted thousands of years and that we haven't been able to overcome yet.

In His Image and Likeness

While the Roman Empire was disintegrating, the Christian religion was preparing to become the new Western social common sense.

Ethics based on compassion and forgiveness should have given life to an ideal society, but instead, it produced the Middle Ages (5th–16th century AD).

The Roman world had not provided great conceptual tools to compare human beings with nonhumans and the environment: neither from a philosophical perspective nor from a legal perspective.

The "power = right" equivalence was sufficiently rooted in the pragmatic Roman mentality not to require justifications or explanations.

Christianity had developed the concept of anthropocentrism, opposed to the ancient Orphic cults, which had some connotations in common with the Roman social order.

Compared to pagans, Christians declared that they aspired to equality among all men but subordinating the latter to God and the rest of creation to themselves.

The Christian man is the center of creation, and everything orbits around him: in this perspective, both the environment and the animals only represent means and not recipients.

Unfortunately, this perspective is strongly rooted in Western civilization, ending up next to the principles of strength and violence typical of the Roman era.

Only human beings resemble the divine and own an eternal soul that would allow them to have expectations about the afterlife.

According to the Christian theology currents of thought, God's sons and daughters can freely and limitlessly dispose of everything that is not human, or they have been forced to be respectful because of the consideration that everything is a divine creation, although it is useful to men.

In both cases, the dominant point of view is that human beings are masters and judges of the destiny of others, with the only possibility to choose to be either cruel or compassionate.

Lights and Shadows

The Age of Enlightenment (eighteenth century) represented the emancipation from religious superstition, marking the return to free thought, to the principles of democracy, of substantial equality (not just declared by words) and guided and inspired an epochal change that seemed to announce a social, cultural, and mental change.

Unfortunately, that change soon vanished, but rather than disappearing, it combined with the Western culture, which was already the result of the mixture of Roman and Christian ideals.

Since the Enlightenment rejected superstition, it also accepted the confusion between spirituality and religion, which had been felt as normal by the common mentality after a millennium of Christianity.

Science and materialism fought anything that transcended human senses, so the label of "superstition" was used to distinguish indiscriminately and by mistake the entire existence that the ancient philosophers had investigated in deep and had the transcendent, the invisible, and the immaterial as the main object.

One of the most negative effects of the Age of Enlightenment was considering religion and spirituality as one and denying the latter by condemning the first.

The philosophy of the Age of Enlightenment created and strengthened a dichotomy that now, paradoxically, nourishes that same sense of human supremacy that had pervaded the Christian thought: however, this time, the source of power and importance is no longer God, but the mind.

The outcome of the Enlightenment revolution was technological and, of course, anthropocentric.

None of the main post-Enlightenment normative codifications shows attention to something that is not human: on the contrary, we see a celebration of the individual, of his specificities, of his freedoms, of his person.

In the long term, the impact of the Enlightenment represents the compendium between the Roman and Christian worlds: not a real revolution of these two, but their evolution.

It is difficult to sum up the Enlightenment Age and all its major exponents: it would be enough to say that many of the most important ones took critical distances from anthropocentrism, even going so far as to point out the importance of respect for nonhumans and, sometimes, the practice of vegetarianism.[11]

According to the Western cultural background, the break between material and immaterial caused an underlying inconsistency in their meanings, leading to materialism and industrial society. This process is destroying the world in the name of profit: another declination of anthropocentrism.

The Anthropocentrism of Opulence

If in the past anthropocentrism came from or was justified by reasons that were ideological or cultural, we can say that in the last century, we have slipped into a "de facto anthropocentrism," characterized by choices that are mostly simply unaware, rather than ideologically oriented.

On the one hand, human rights, many of which don't relate to fundamental needs or interests, are increasingly spreading. But, on the other hand, anthropocentrism led to a new set of rights for equal dignity to everybody because any right was granted to what is not human.

For example, in the ancient world, animals were exploited for food or transport purposes. Now they are used for painful pharmaceutical and cosmetic tests, developing new weapons, vehicles, or the "race to space." Regarding the environment, in the past, humans impacted the environment to build houses, roads, or to provide heating, while today threats are more dangerous than ever: atomic tests, overbuilding, chemicals in agriculture, illegal dumps in the name of mere profit.

All these circumstances seem to be consistent with the evolutionary direction of our species. However, it is proof of our moral schizophrenia, considering that we are experiencing the first legislation about environmental and animal issues, completely unknown in the past.

Although our terminology and laws could suggest a conceptual overcoming of anthropocentrism, some facts reveal the opposite; it would be misleading to think of an anthropocentric cultural inclination greater now than in the past because daily choices of people show how they believe to be superior to all other living species, despite ideological assumptions of superiority declined.

Anthropocentrism is not based on cultural background, and, therefore, it can be defeated only on a practical level. So how could we do that? First of all, rejecting behaviors that damage or suppress fundamental interests: capturing a lion for the pleasure of observing it in a zoo or clearing forests to create a golf club are good examples.

The consumerist society cannot help but promote an opulent model of life in which, having now satisfied the real needs, the individual – no longer a "person" but a "consumer" – must be induced to experience desire and a sense of need toward objects that are excessive for him and harmful to everyone else (often also being harmful to him).

In a world where economic interest has risen to supreme divinity, everything else must be enslaved. It is easier to enslave those who have no voice and cannot rebel, such as nonhuman animals and the environment. This perspective is not even anthropocentric: in the logic of profit, defenseless humans are also commodified and deprived of rights.

The only method to counter this new phenomenon is to contrast the culture of money and consumption with respect and personal and collective evolution. But, unfortunately, the media pressure and the omnipresent advertising industry represent a difficult obstacle to overcome.

1.3 ANIMAL ADVOCACY AND ANTISPECIESISM

Alongside the anthropocentric culture that has characterized most Western history, alternative or complementary proposals have emerged in more recent times, focusing on nonhuman animals.

These currents of thought represent the overcoming of previous limits: the attempt to broaden the views, overcoming the typical and intrinsic prejudice of anthropocentrism.

The cultural and philosophical movement in the defense of animals is a very recent phenomenon, often traced back to Singer's Animal Liberation publication from 1975.

In this work, while considering the different currents of thought and the critical issues related to the definition of animal advocacy, I decided to keep this term in its wide and inclusive meaning of associationism and "popular culture" phenomena and philosophical thought.

Despite all the distinctions of meanings we can make about it, we can keep using this term, especially when referring to that thought that aims to claim respect and protection for animals.

According to all the supporters of the terminology above, it is not correct to use the concept of "animal rights"; it is quite controversial because those who consider it a superfluous or even a harmful label to animal liberation from human exploitation do actually claim that animals' interests have to be recognized. Such recognition, even if not called "right," is clearly connected with rig.[12]

Many thinkers have different ideas on the matter, but the three most important contemporary ones are Peter Singer, Tom Regan, and Gary L. Francione.

First of all, a false myth must be dispelled: animal rights activists do not place animals on a higher level than humans: none of the philosophical exponents of animal advocacy has ever supported this approach.

Many animal rights activists disagree about placing animals and humans on the same level.

According to some activists and exponents of animal advocacy (Regan and Francione in particular), it would be necessary to establish *animal rights* to protect nonhumans. Some others don't give importance to this issue or just don't consider it.

The right represents a specific technical institute and is often used in a nontechnical sense, which can be described as "recognizing something to someone."

All exponents of philosophical animal advocacy attribute to animals' higher importance than nature and the environment.

Animals are considered comparable to one another according to biological and logical reasoning; analytical discussions on scientific topics are often debated in books about animal advocacy to support the animal/human analogy.

The Limits of Utilitarianism

Utilitarianism undoubtedly stands out among the moral theories that have extended their consideration outside of humanity, starting with its founder, the English philosopher Jeremy Bentham, who considered the ability of nonhuman animals to suffer an index of reference of morality, concluding that it must necessarily include all those who can experience well-being and suffering.[13]

Peter Singer, a utilitarian, applied Bentham's moral to the relationship between different species. He says that the well-being deriving to humans from meat consumption is not comparable to the suffering inflicted on nonhumans; therefore, according to the utilitarian principle of maximizing global welfare, it is necessary to stop eating practices involving animal suffering.[14]

Based on the same considerations, Singer reaches similar conclusions also concerning issues other than food, similarly rejecting medical and cosmetic tests, hunting, and such.

Utilitarianism, in and of itself, does not imply any precept of conduct toward nonhuman animals. However, utilitarian scholars state that all animals (not only humans) are capable of suffering, and for this reason, they must be considered in the same way.

There is a first, evident limit in the utilitarian theory, which aspires to be all-encompassing and nonspecific, but inevitably ends up falling back into prejudice: How do you know who suffers and who does not suffer? And, again, how can suffering or pleasure be compared?

In very general and generic terms, it is obvious that life and the palate's satisfaction are issues light-years away, but how far can certainties be pushed in this regard? For example, a pig raised outdoors and killed without stress does not feel suffering, while those who feed on it feel satisfaction: is this therefore justifiable?

Also, which animal species experience suffering? Do insects prove it? Which species would therefore be usable, as they are incapable of suffering?

In short, utilitarian animal advocacy presupposes:

- Scientific certainties about who can suffer.
- Comparability of the levels of suffering and satisfaction.
- Lawfulness of conduct which, even if resulting in exploitation or disposition of others, does not imply suffering.[15]

The above is not reflected in the fact that scientific knowledge is limited and strictly dependent on the historical era and that, therefore, not only is it impossible to establish with certainty who may suffer, but neither is it possible to understand which suffering is worse, nor which fulfillment is better. The further limitation of this theory does not know the exact thoughts and perceptions of others. Therefore, it is possible to justify a series of behaviors that, in our opinion, would not cause suffering but which would result in operative acts such as detention, control of populations, and such.

It took millennia of human evolution to establish sciences capable of identifying certain animal behaviors and understanding the psychological consequences of actions such as confinement in confined spaces, separation from the like, and such.

A moral principle based on partial and limited information can only turn out to be partial and limited, and therefore erroneous, in the sense that the logical conclusion of these premises is the adoption of approximate behaviors, which could become "perfect" (according to the utilitarian definition) only when our knowledge was absolute, unlimited, and shared by all.

Historically, utilitarianism should be recognized as the first formulation of a moral theory, including nonhuman animals; nevertheless, it seems that its leading exponents have sometimes reached contradictory conclusions concerning the inspiring principles. Nevertheless, the warning to take into consideration the interests of nonhumans is certainly valid and acceptable, although erroneously limited to animals: the paradigm of suffering can be useful concerning the prohibition of procuring it, but the existence itself becomes—especially from Singer—considered undeserving of protection, or, at least, of respect.

The main merit of utilitarianism is to bring to the agent's attention the concrete repercussions of his actions on the "neighbor," thus imposing not to adopt behaviors that, in compliance with any abstract principles, end up damaging the other by himself. Avoiding others' damages should be the basis for any moral doctrine, and Eusebism recognizes it.

The Limits of Deontologism

Another current of animal advocate philosophy is based on deontology, which is opposed to utilitarianism as it does not accept to relativize the criterion of "rights" concerning the satisfaction of agents, believing instead that, if the conduct is right, it must be regardless of the benefit that can derive from it and that, therefore, it must be implemented "whatever it costs."

Even deontology starts from the suffering of animals, opposing any treatment that may cause it; however, this current of thought is not limited to what is normally identified as welfare, instead of going so far as to claim the emanation of real animal rights and the end of exploitation.

The expression "animal rights" does not indicate anything in particular, but is used to encompass many ways with different shades in which a set of nonhuman interests and expectations are intended to be protected.

Animal rights are unknown to utilitarianism, or, at least, hardly compatible with its moral formulations, as it could also be about human rights. When their recognition involved greater deprivation or inconvenience (such as merchants and slave masters), there would be no reason to set them up.

The founder of the ethical philosophy is Immanuel Kant, who, regarding the human/nonhuman relationship, had stated, "If he is not to stifle his human feelings, he must practice kindness toward animals, for he who is cruel to animals becomes hard also in his dealings with men."[16] It is a completely subjective prospect, which is also the basis of the so-called "indirect duties" toward animals, which conceal duties toward their fellow humans.[17]

Kant's thesis is currently the most accepted in Western legal systems, aiming to punish harmful behaviors toward animals as harmful to humans, heritage, and feelings.

Like utilitarianism, deontologism does not take into consideration beings different from humans either. For this reason, the environment and animals can alternatively be included or excluded from deontologist moral theories.

Tom Regan and the Subjects-of-a-life

The leading exponent of animal rights ethics was Tom Regan, who focused on the principle of respect, developing the concept of the *subject-of-a-life*: all those who belong to this category are to be considered recipients of respect for others automatically.

Subjects-of-a-life, according to Regan, are all mammals over one year of age in normal conditions of development, and it is this category, which he invented, that acts as a discriminant for his moral theory. However, the same philosopher says he is aware of the difficulties one runs into when trying to determine the minimum threshold of self-determination and self-awareness and concludes that it is preferable to err by excess rather than by default.[18]

To clear the field of misunderstandings, Regan carries out a comparative human-animal analysis, intended to demonstrate that both have intellectual faculties and beliefs and desires: this would represent the foundation of real interests worthy of protection.

In this way, the philosophical passage from indirect duties to direct duties toward animals is perfected and, therefore, claims fundamental rights for the latter.

This perspective also shows insuperable limits.

First, we are starting from the human perspective of reality: it is up to man to evaluate and distinguish between kingdoms and species. The determination of the intellectual faculties or individuals' mental and moral capacities is left to their appreciation. From this point of view, the rights of nonhumans would remain a concession on the part of humans because similarities are recognized between "us" and "them."

Those who do not resemble us, those who are not a mammal, or even an animal, cannot have rights as they cannot even be considered a subject or a person in a philosophical-juridical sense.

There is also an intrinsic limit in Regan's considerations, which, on the one hand, outlines the category of subjects-of-a-life, and, on the other hand, affirms that respect should not be due exclusively to those who belong to it. This, in my opinion, underlines how it is a completely arbitrary category, so much so that the author himself ends up depleting it of relevance and ultimately admitting its randomness.

An example is useful to clarify Regan's contradictions: comparing humans and nonhumans, he figures a conflict emerging in a lifeboat carrying four men and a dog that requires throwing an individual into the sea to save the others.

The premises of Regan's philosophy would lead us to believe that the choice cannot be to save humans at the dog's expense. At the same time, this is the precise conclusion that he reaches instead, stating that greater damage would occur by sacrificing the human being. This is an evident logical distortion, which finds no explanation concerning the presuppositions of his thought, nor can he find any. Would it be more harmful to save a Labrador who rescues humans or a human being? Who could trigger a war? Would it be fairer to sacrifice a puppy dog with a peaceful life expectancy or a terminally ill human?

In short, it is difficult to recognize any absolute prerequisite for issuing a value judgment such that it can be concluded that it is "always" better to sacrifice one or the other. However, Regan's thought is a philosophy which, although pioneering in many respects and certainly decisive in the debate on animal rights, does not aim to define relationships within the same species such as between men, nor does it consider it possible to take all which is considered life into consideration, let alone the rest.

Gary Francione and the Abolitionist Approach

Gary Francione prefers Regan's vision of rights against so-called welfarism, a typical expression of many legislative policies pursued in Western countries since the nineteenth century. Embracing Regan's ideas, Francione also concludes that welfarism, as an expression of substantial utilitarianism, would not guarantee effective protection for nonhuman animals.[19]

According to Francione, human animals would approach their nonhuman peers from a perspective of utility and exploitation. For this reason, they freely and unscrupulously dispose of animals to get food, to have fun, or to dress, and such. Francione says that this approach derives from the fact that historically animals have been considered an indicator of wealth by man and, therefore, mere properties at the same level as any other material good. Francione points out the etymology of some words, such as the Latin pecunia (money), having a common root to pecus (sheep), and the English cattle (livestock), having the same root as the word capital.[20]

Francione also affirms the principle of equal consideration of interests, which requires abandoning any conception, such as those based on sex, race, species, and such. On these bases, the author goes beyond theories by Regan, stating that limitation based on subjects-of-a-life has no raison d'etre once animals are recognized as subjects rather than objects.

Francione's approach, which disregards the comparison between the cognitive abilities of the various species and equates all sentient life forms as recipients of the duty of respect, probably represents the most recent innovative contribution to the theory of animal rights.

Francione is a pure abolitionist, who does not consider any intermediate way to guarantee the rights of animals feasible, if not—in fact—the abolition of all forms of exploitation and not only those that involve suffering or killing.

According to Francione, the reformist laws are wrong and harmful, as they cannot lead to the end of animal exploitation, while they make people more comfortable with it, thinking that there is no unnecessary or undue suffering.[21]

The main difference between Regan and Francione lies in the fact that the latter extends the categories of animals subject to law formulated by the former, stating that there are no reasons to limit them to subjects-of-a-life.

Francione argues that speciesism does not differ from other discriminatory attitudes. Therefore, animal rights activists cannot be consistent if they do not stand against such thought forms.

Francione's thought is either incomplete or contradictory: he takes into consideration human and nonhuman animals. He affirms that any discrimination is to be tried again, but in excluding both nonanimal life forms and the environment in general, he proves to carry out discrimination. Moreover, it is not clear what this discrimination is based on: insects, for example, are certainly alive, but they are not included among those deemed worthy of legal protection.

More precisely, Francione emphasizes that the excuse in the attribution of the fundamental right not to be treated as an instrument for others lies in possession of a sentient nature and in the ability to lead an experiential life through the senses. This ability abstractly connects it to all animals, starting from the assumption that sentient nature is the right path followed by nature to allow survival by avoiding pain, hunger, seeking fulfillment, reproduction, and such.

Francione says,

> Although there may be cases in which it is not clear whether a being is sentient, such as about insects or mollusks, most of the nonhuman animals we exploit are undoubtedly self-conscious and have an interest in continuing to exist, even if they do not have the same self-awareness that we associate with normal humans.[22]

There are some "shadows" in this thought, that are the main limitation of Francione's thesis:

i) a (subjective) assessment about who is sentient,
ii) discrimination against those who are not (deemed) sentient,
iii) a contradiction concerning the premises.

Who is sentient? Who is not? The decision is uncertain and arbitrary, being based on limited and imprecise science.[23] Such a decision is another discrimination, not unlike those contested and accused of "speciesism."

The most evident contradiction in Francione's thesis is that, while it correctly recognizes the right of those who suffer not to suffer (better to say: of those who have the aptitude for suffering), it fails to recognize the right to exist of those who exist, or the right to live of those who live.

Saying that only sentient beings can accrue interests worthy of protection is, still, an anthropocentric perspective.

What aspires to be defined as "right" can, in principle, be considered to coincide with what is necessary. Abolishing "all" discriminations is very different from disputing "some." For this reason, the most logical consequence of Francione's arguments would be to refrain from indiscriminately disposing of even those who are not human or animal and, therefore, extending the protection even to different forms of existence.

Another criticality emerges about feeding pets: Francione states that it is permissible to use animal foods since it is a need. It is indeed possible to recognize humans' moral duty toward domestic nonhumans – if they are animals stolen from death or mistreatment for human causes and in any case excluding any specimen purchased – but it is also true that in deciding to sacrifice one for another, we discriminate. Humanity, in general, has moral duties to help and provide sustenance toward those nonhumans that it has led to the existence or who, in any case, has distorted, deprived of habitat, and exposed to mistreatment, unnatural dangers, and such.

Therefore, not helping those animals represents an (indirect) injury to their interests.

Using other animals to feed pets is a direct injury: we decide whom to sacrifice and whom to save, not just by merely watching but also by acting in the first person.

There can be no moral legitimacy in deciding to save the one to whom one is attached, condemning those we do not know: not even the responsibility toward that subject can legitimize us to carry out dispositive acts toward others.

Beyond Antiracism

Antispeciesism is a current thought that arose around the definition "speciesism," coined in 1975 by the American psychiatrist Richard W. Ryder.[24]

In the description of its creator, speciesist behavior would represent discrimination not unlike the more well-known ones such as racism, sexism, and such, with the only difference being belonging to a species.

Some proponents of this thought gave it an extensive interpretation, including banning any discriminatory behavior and not only speciesist behaviors. This so-called political antiracism also compares humans to animals and the environment.

It is my opinion that, in an attempt to invent something new at all costs, antispeciesism created something that can exist just in connection with its opposite (speciesism).

Meanwhile, in acting out of racism or sexism, there is a manifest and systematic will, which is not innate but rooted or deliberate: one chooses, for example, to systematically suppress individuals of a race as they are considered inferior or simply harmful compared to another race. Species discrimination is quite another thing: in nature, any species that compete with other species does so involuntarily but inevitably are induced to recognize the interest of their kind as prevalent over that of members of other species.

In arbitrarily disposing of everything that is not human, man does not move from an ethical reason. Still, he limits himself to letting himself go to an instinct, where – moreover – none of the persecutory behaviors that characterize the other "isms" cited above happen.

We do not kill tens of billions of nonhuman animals every year because we hate them, but simply because we put our interest as individuals before their interest. Unfortunately, in most cases, this is not done directly by consumers but by a few producers who scrupulously conceal the reality that, for example, divides a cow from a hamburger.

For many people, eating other animals means to fulfill a need. For them, it is not a question of discriminating between humans and nonhumans but of doing what even the lion does with the gazelle.

Many consider zoos a place where animals are housed, cared for, and safeguarded from the dangerous wild nature, the sale of dogs as a normal form of trade for man's best friend, and so on.

In my opinion, no one can be accused, if not the "few" who base their economic gain on the exploitation of animals and of deliberate discrimination of species.

Instead, we should reason, rather than as part of the "antispeciesist problem," as part of its solution: which antispeciesist can guarantee the same treatment to human, nonhuman animals (including insects), plants, and such?

Suppose we want to be considered antispeciesist. In that case, we cannot make distinctions between any animal species.

Who pays the same attention to a human hit by a car rather than a bird or a wasp? We accept to take a plane or a train that will kill thousands of insects, we drive cars that do the same, and we often walk without caring that under our weight, perhaps in the grass, dozens of insects are overwhelmed and crushed, perhaps left to agonize: is all this antispeciesist? If it were, then it would be a completely contradictory and unusable definition. Still, it is easy to see that one cannot argue that in everyday life, we take it for granted that each "entity," and therefore each species, has different relevance.

And what about vegetables? What if they weren't species different from ours that we consider exploitable for the most disparate reasons? Perhaps we would be willing to kill a person as easily as we uproot a tree to build a house? Maybe we would exterminate hordes of humans to produce paper for our printed words?

In short, just as speciesism does not exist, neither does its opposite. How could something that is not subject to any description or systematic classification exist? In my opinion, the so-called antispeciesism is just an attempt to codify conduct, not based on conscious choice but innate instincts, cultural contaminations, and factual circumstances.

Antispeciesism could exist only if speciesism existed, but once the latter is abolished, what would the world build? The abolition of condemned behavior can only represent a single facet of a broader program. Otherwise, it is bound to run out together with what it disputes.

The fact that we are antispeciesists affects only the human/nonhuman relationship: What about everything else? What about intraspecies relations? Many people claim that being antispeciesist also implies adopting other principles about life and relations, but this is completely subjective.

Although carried by some movements far beyond what it represents, this definition will always remain confined to the context that produced it.

Also, to adopt an "anti" definition means to focus on the problem we are trying to solve, somehow recalling and promoting it. It is a dualist perspective that does not allow grey areas: you are supposed to be for or against; no third ways.

It would be much more appropriate to assume autonomous definitions, capable of evoking in anyone a new and completely different thought that does not lie in the shadow of its opposite.

Designing a different world stopping at the criticism of the existing one would be like governing a country, just based on foreign policy and with the sole purpose of overturning the previous government, but without any plans regarding any other issues. This is a dangerous strategy because you will realize that you are good to fight at the end of the day, not to govern.

In conclusion, if you just want to fight against something, then "anti" movements are suitable to you; if, on the other hand, you want to build something different, then you should probably think of something broader.

1.4 ECOLOGISM AND BIOCENTRISM

Ecologism is not different from so-called animal advocacy, at least, in its criticism against anthropocentrism. Thus, it is no coincidence that concern for the environment became systematic and organized in the twentieth century in conjunction with the spread of industrial society and the worsening of the visible consequences.

At least initially, the "movement" was not based on philosophical bases but rather on safeguarding people's habitat: a survival instinct. This resulted in the absence of a defined conceptual framework, an instrumental and only apparent interest in the environment. Actually, this movement is aimed to safeguard nature as a means of survival for man.

We can call this movement "instrumental environmentalism" (or shallow ecology), referring to the fact that its final goal is to protect human beings and their quality of life.

In short, the phenomenon of environmentalism has branched out, taking on political and philosophical connotations and determining the birth of many organized groups, active in different sectors and on different issues, including not only "infrastructure" (the planet and habitat), but also some of its inhabitants, in particular, wild animals (or some of them).

Instrumental environmentalism in politics gave birth to many green parties, promoting the protection of human health and future generations.

Biocentrism has gone "beyond" animal advocacy and intended to remove species barriers, including those between the animal and plant kingdom, turning its attention to all living beings.

We can see that the same definition of what is alive or not is controversial. This is because it has had to continually adapt to scientific advances in history, while it is still impossible for us to understand where our definition of "life" came from.

According to Darwin, by "origin of life," we mean:

> The first appearance of living entities. Suppose the emergence of the biosphere is seen as the evolutionary transition between the nonliving and the living. In that case, it may be meaningless to attempt to draw a strict line between these two worlds, and the appearance of life on Earth may therefore be better envisioned as a continuum that seamlessly joins the prebiotic synthesis and accumulation of organic molecules in the primitive environment with the emergence of self-sustaining, replicative chemical systems capable of undergoing Darwinian evolution.[25]

Although this distinction is the result of an arbitrary classification, in the same way, scholars debate whether viruses can be qualified as forms of life or not.

Since our understanding of reality is limited, so are our conclusions: we do not know where the so-called life originated, and our analysis is incomplete and fallacious.

An increasingly large number of scholars are turning in favor of theories that include everything that lives within a single system: these theories are flawed in origin, at least until the origin of life is understood, and therefore a correct and absolute answer will not be given to the question "What is alive?"

First, when we talk about life, we imply the adjective "terrestrial." Yet, so far, ours is the only planet where official science claims any life is, and it cannot hypothesize if there are any extraterrestrial entities.

It is currently said that the first living beings originated from the primordial soup, which is "*a mixture of organic molecules in evolutionary theory from which life on earth originated.*"[26]

In 1924, the Russian chemist Alexander Oparin hypothesized that this jumble of substances was made possible by the chemical reactions produced and favored by the primordial atmosphere, devoid of oxygen but rich in water, ammonia, and methane. However, the experiments since then have never led to any artificial reproduction of protocells.[27]

Oparin is still the most accredited scientific theory on the origin of terrestrial life. In contrast, an alternative theory is known as panspermia (from the Greek πᾶν, "all" + σπέρμα, "seed"): in 1908, the Swedish chemist Arrhenius formulated the hypothesis that meteorites and comets had carried microbes inside them, which survived in the space and then colonized the Earth.[28]

While providing an interpretation about the possible origin of life on Earth, the theory of panspermia says nothing about its true origin. Instead, it merely transfers the primal phenomenon from ours to other planets (or parts of the Universe).

In short, what is alive will remain doubtful, at least until it is clear what life is, and at that point, we can perhaps discuss the fact that the difference between the two conditions can ground discrimination.

Ecosophy or Deep Ecology

Deep ecology, or ecosophy, was founded in 1973 by the Norwegian philosopher Arne Naess.[29] This thought rejects instrumental environmentalism by recognizing the intrinsic value of the environment, or, better to say, of the "ecosystem."

Ecosophy is to the environmental movement what animal rights are to welfarism. In short, if protesting to prevent the cutting of trees placed in front of your house, which provide shade and decorate the landscape, is the paradigm of environmentalism (or shallow ecology), taking action to protect the existence of a tree from the other side of the world is deep ecology.

In his essay on deep ecology, Naess rejected " *man-in-environment image in favor of the relational total field image.*" Shallow ecology was described as "*against pollution and the exploitation of resources*" aimed at protecting "*the health and well-being of the inhabitants of developed countries.*"[30]

Naess argued that biospheric egalitarianism must inspire the relationship between humans and all other forms of life, specifying that "*any realistic conduct implies some killing, exploitation, and suppression.*"[31] I believe that there are already two misunderstandings in this definition.

First, one cannot speak of "exploitation" where an entity complies with its nature. If, for example, a wolf devours an herbivore, in the holistic view of ecosophy, this action should be considered instrumental in maintaining global balance, not an end or for the well-being of the wolf. Suppose there is the maintenance of balance and, therefore, compliance with one's functions. In that case, there can be no exploitation because considering it would mean disregarding the function of an element within the broader context to which it belongs. It is about a non-negligible internal contradiction.

The second criticality, in my opinion, is that Naess takes for granted the need of killing without demonstrating it in any way, thus merely accepting the belief that humans are omnivorous, and therefore considering it natural and right that they kill other animals to feed on them. Again, however, I believe that there was an underlying simplism in considering only "the living," failing to identify specifically "who" they are and neglecting to include that it is the human being who coined the term "life," and therefore determined whom to include or exclude.

The deep ecology platform was summarized by Arne Naess and George Sessions in eight points:

1. The well-being and flourishing of human and nonhuman life on Earth have value in themselves (synonyms: inherent worth, intrinsic value, inherent value). These values are independent of the usefulness of the nonhuman world for human purposes.
2. Richness and diversity of life forms contribute to the realization of these values and are also values in themselves.
3. Humans have no right to reduce this richness and diversity except to satisfy vital needs.
4. Present human interference with the nonhuman world is excessive, and the situation is rapidly worsening.
5. The flourishing of human life and cultures is compatible with a substantial decrease of the human population. The flourishing of nonhuman life requires such a decrease.
6. Policies must therefore be changed. The changes in policies affect basic economic, technological, and ideological structures. The resulting state of affairs will be deeply different from the present.

7. The ideological change is mainly that of appreciating life quality (dwelling in situations of inherent worth) rather than adhering to an increasingly higher standard of living. There will be a profound awareness of the difference between big and great.
8. Those who subscribe to the foregoing points have an obligation directly or indirectly to participate in the attempt to implement the necessary changes.[32]

Ecosophy has its roots in the perennial philosophy, which is the thought transversal to philosophers, mystics, religious, and even scientists that considers the substantial connection of the whole as a fundamental characteristic of existence.[33] Pythagoras and Plato are two of the main exponents of the perennial philosophy. Both largely based their works on metaphysics and the soul's reincarnation and the afterlife (or hyperuranium).[34] In Naess, the concept of biocentrism, or biocentric equality, is the equalization of all forms of life as endowed with intrinsic value, assumes great importance. This represents an overcoming of the anthropocentric concept and the zoocentric one, with the view of a new horizon.

Overcoming anthropocentrism – Naess states – implies the process of self-realization and the acquisition of the awareness of belonging to an inseparable context that includes all living beings.

Leading representatives of deep ecology, in addition to Naess, are Jon Krakauer, David Thoreau, and Aldo Leopold.

Leopold's essay, *Thinking Like a Mountain*,[35] explains ecosophy's view about the man-animal-environment relationship. First, the author describes the episode of wolf hunting in which, seeing pain and anger in the eyes of the dying animal, he understood the effects of his gesture. This reflection was then added to the observation that herbivore animals, in the absence of natural predators, cause an imbalance in the environment that damages humans.

Leopold's reflection highlights a conception quite distant from the concept of animal rights, and it looks somehow incomplete. As for the first aspect, Leopold clearly fails to consider the individual perspective, thus failing to give relevance to the individual's suffering and the frustration of his expectations.

What is relevant, if anything, is the organic dimension within which individuals and groups act and in which they take on a value that it would be misleading to define as intrinsic. It is an extrinsic value whose usefulness toward man is not direct but rather indirect. It is in this last reflection that I see superficiality, or immaturity, in Leopold's thought: if, on the one hand, he claims the dignity of all living beings, regardless of their usefulness for human beings (or the damage they can cause them), on the other hand, it ends up reaffirming its value on the same basis, that is, utility. According to

Leopold's reasoning, one would conclude that it is not true that living beings must be respected regardless of utility. Still, that real utility would come from letting them live without interference.

Based on Leopold's assumptions, we should conclude that it is not permissible to kill the wolf if its death damages the environment (e.g., because there are too many herbivore animals). Otherwise, nothing will hinder the environment or even be necessary (e.g., if the human being had already killed most of the prey). This concept ends up excluding, from the general duty of respect, all those who, by nature or by supervening facts, are not "useful" to the environment they participate in.

The ecocentric principle underlying ecosophy emerges above all in the food issue: nonhuman animals are conceived as "expendable" in the name of a concept of global balance and as a sort of natural life which, complying with the canon that predators are feeding on prey, would allow you to kill for your use.

It is here that the theory of animal rights and ecosophy reach the point of maximum detachment, starting from that initial difference that leads the first to dwell on the intrinsic value of the individual and the second to consider its usefulness in the broader context and global.[36]

The claim of deep ecology to attribute intrinsic value to any living being clashes with a blatant omission of the philosophical criterion, which should ground this respect in opposition to utilitarianism. Although formally the idea that the dignity of individuals (or of groups) derives from their usefulness, substantially, this seems to be the only justification underlying the concept of "ecosystem."

By better connecting some considerations of ecosophy with the premises, a more coherent basis of thought could be defined: the subjectivity of the observation and the partiality underlying its judgment imply that any attempt to discriminate in any way based on belonging to categories, which are also arbitrary, is both fallacious and flawed.

Ecosophy describes the organic functioning of a natural world, which is considered a starting and ending point. Within that "natural" model, all the elements participate in the functioning of a higher mechanism. The intrinsic value attributed to them derives precisely from this functional necessity. However, this could not be said about animals produced by humans for their ends that do not fit into a virtuous or natural circle. Indeed, on closer inspection, the enormous quantity of animals produced for human purposes (which for food alone is about 60 billion individuals each year) determines an imbalance of the ecosphere, compromising its functioning and even threatening its survival. In this context, as with predators in nature, ecosophy should consider killing nonhuman animals not only lawful but even necessary.

I do not believe that the typical criticism of ecosophy, which is accused of submitting man to nature, is correct. Considering all life forms as a "part of the whole" is remarkable, but, in deep ecology, it ends up neglecting specificities.

Deep ecology provides an interpretation of the Universe as being in some ways "profound" and, at the same time, extremely superficial and incomplete. One of the philosophical premises of this thought is the repudiation of finalism. I agree with this general statement, but I do not think it can represent the justification for renouncing the deeper understanding of the nature of things and their eventual finalist, which may well disregard human purposes.

If humans and the Universe are connected, understanding the origin of one means understanding that of the other. The theory is an unfinished attempt if we miss such preliminary understanding because it lacks the proper tools.

In conclusion, deep ecology represents a trend full of fundamental ideas and reflections, which, if shared, would undoubtedly lead to a more balanced and respectful world. Unfortunately, however, its serious gaps and some profound contradictions end up relegating it to the rank of stimulus, valid to assist other conceptions but unable to stand as a complete formulation of a moral system or even as a reference in all facets of existence.

One of the main limitations of ecosophy is its antithetical nature to industrial society: if we start negating a model, our thought will be limited.

The ecosophical approach offers many ideas for the transformation of contemporary society. Still, it would not have provided any (or at least, only negligible) indication of conduct in a preindustrial society, nor could it offer any to a postindustrial one.

In short, deep ecology seems like an excellent beginning and a framework from which to start to move from more general considerations to more specific ones, thus combining "the whole" with the individual and allowing to fully develop concepts that have remained unresolved or even contradictory, for example by incorporating concepts of gradation of the damage.

The holistic conception of the Universe proposed by ecosophy is a common part of Eusebism, which, however, goes further, not limiting the object of attention to the man-ecosystem relationship and posing the question of single individuals' interindividual relationships. This happens not under the presumption of real and substantial separation between individuals but by taking note of the peculiarities which, although apparent, are nevertheless functional to existence itself and therefore cannot be neglected.

Biocentrism According to Robert Lanza

Biocentric (from the Greek βίος, life + κέντρον, center) are those theories that place life at the center of moral consideration. This current of thought represents an extension concerning that of the rights or protection of animals since it exceeds the limit underlying it of being addressed only by certain living beings. More precisely, biocentrism abolishes the barrier between animal and vegetable kingdoms.

Concerning ecologism, be it superficial or deep, there is an apparent restriction since the nonliving beings are excluded from consideration. This concept appeared around the 1970s without finding any conceptual collocation or organic arrangement.

Robert Lanza (1956) is an MD, particularly successful in stem cell research, who in 2007 formulated a theory called biocentrism based on a mixture of observations, data, and theories deriving from medicine, chemistry, and physics.[37]

Lanza's main work on the subject is *biocentrism.* The book was coauthored by the astronomer Bob Berman is entitled.[38] After reviewing some examples and different theories of quantum physics, Lanza formulates his description of the Universe, concluding that life is not the result of the latter but the opposite.

The core of biocentrism is based on seven principles.

1) What we perceive as reality is a process that involves our awareness.
2) Our external and internal perceptions are inextricably interconnected. They represent different sides of the same coin and cannot be separated from each other.
3) The behavior of subatomic particles: all particles and objects are linked to the presence of an observer. Without a conscious observer, at most, they can exist in the indeterminate state of probability waves.
4) "Matter" is in an indeterminate state of probability.
   Any universe that may have preceded awareness would have existed only in a state of probability.
5) The structure of the Universe can only be explained through biocentrism. The Universe is calibrated on life, perfectly consistent with how life created the Universe, not the other way around. Thus, the "universe" is simply the overall spatial-temporal logic of the individual.
6) Time has no real existence outside the perception of the animal senses. It is the process by which we perceive the changes in the Universe.
7) Space, like time, is not an object or a thing. Space represents another form in our understanding as animals and is not an independent reality.[39]

Lanza's formulation is much more focused on science than philosophy. Thus, his analysis focuses mainly on the mechanics of the Universe rather than on his interpretation.

In this case, the centrality of life is not a philosophical premise but rather a fact. From that fact, we should conclude that biology represents the key to knowledge. Lanza invites physicists and chemists to review their positions to use biology, particularly neuroscience, as the lowest common denominator in analyzing both the individual and the entire Universe.

The author's position seems unresolved or, at least, unfinished. In the face of a comparative analysis of different sciences, an infrastructure of thought is completely missing.

In short, Lanza's biocentrism—at least in the current state of things—is not a scientific theory, as it lacks a formulation of this type. On the other hand, however, it is not a philosophical theory either: if anything, it is a transversal operation aimed at collecting the state of the art of different disciplines, linking it with the observation of everyday facts, even trivial ones.

Trying to formulate the philosophical conclusions of Lanza's scientific premises, one could imagine at least some main implications, hence an apparent contradiction. First, if it is true that everything exists because of the conscience's will and that it contributes to the realization and sustenance of life, then it is true that there is no real difference between life and nonlife.

The same author specifies that the experience of life persists after the death of the body,[40] thus showing that he conceives existence in a transcendental way, similarly to the main currents of ecosophy.

These are shared premises in Eusebism, which relate to different consequences, trying to overcome the traditional limits underlying them and which prevent the recognition of protection for individuals and the definitive determination of who is to be protected and how.

1.5 THE *REDUCTIO AD UNUM*

Anyone who has driven a car in curves, especially in roundabouts, has experienced the so-called "centrifugal force" phenomenon, pushing toward the outside of the ideal circumference representing motion.

The centrifugal force is apparent: it does not exist because, actually, it is a centripetal force directed toward the center of the circumference.

Our perspective leads us to consider centrifugal force as existing: a flawed, nonobjective perspective. The same happens with psychological or behavioral classifications.

Daily living, on closer inspection, is not based on ideological or idealistic significance but rather on trivial attempts to affirm oneself and one's interests (or those of one's loved ones), overwhelming the other, whomever they are. When, for example, we find ourselves in line for any bureaucratic fulfillment, we do not want to be the first in line because we despise others who are doing the same process, but simply because we consider them obstacles to our interest.

Our interest is that we earn more, finish first, have the best house or car, and such. Therefore, it does not upset us that others make good money or have short lines or have nice cars, but that they make more money than we do, make shorter lines, or have better cars.

Most of the claims we make, even when we cloak ourselves with altruism, are an expression of profound selfishness: we become environmentalists when they touch the park in front of our house, animal rights advocates when they beat a puppy in front of us, pro-animal testing on the disease that hit us or our loved ones, and such.

In short, just as the true force is centripetal, even if it appears as centrifugal, so egoism is the profound reason that determines all those behaviors named in various ways due to limited and limiting perspectives.

The evidence is so trivial that it is probably not even considered: a racist toward an ethnic group is never someone who belongs to it, just as one is a speciesist or sexist always toward the "other."

Society is not speciesist, racist, and sexist: it is simply selfish.

The effects of rampant selfishness manifest in small and big things: from smoking to buying useless goods without considering their impact, from eating to drinking to exploiting the weakest, etc.

Subdividing, classifying, schematizing, and partially analyzing this myriad of "isms" is not only useless, but it is seriously harmful. In the first place, it implies the suffrage of a dualist perspective, endorsing the existence of those same differences that are denied.

To fossilize on the different treatment of an indefinite number of issues also implies losing sight of the real problem, preventing us from facing it: this causes fragmentation of energies and confusion on questions that are in themselves simple and monistic.

More recent history is full of examples, often considered noble, of people who have risen to great fame and prestige for having waged important battles against individual manifestations of human selfishness. However, in reality, we should look at these figures as unaware people, or only partially aware, as they can distinguish selfishness toward a human ethnic group, but not that of all humans toward nonhumans, and, indeed, perpetuating it in turn.

Try to figure society as a ship and each "ism" as a leak in the hull. In that case, we see how complex and unlikely it is to seal them all completely by focusing on one at a time: our limited awareness leads us to consider those leaks not as symptoms of an already faulty hull but as problems in themselves be solved individually. But when leaks continually open in the hull, we cannot hope for safe navigation: we need to rethink it and intervene on the cause, not on the symptoms.

I believe it is essential to operate a conceptual *reductio ad Unum*, capable of identifying all those concrete conducts that undermine coexistence, respect, and balance, giving up the established compartmentalized system based on symptoms and neglects the causes.

NOTES

1. Levi, Arnold Post, *From Homer to Menander: Forces in Greek Poetic Fiction*, volume 23, University of California Press, 1951, p. 71.
2. J. Shull, Peter, *Non-destructive Evaluation: Theory, Technics, and Application*, CRC Press Book, 2002, p. 28.
3. Anderson, Robert S., Beatty, Richard, *Insects and Spiders of the World*, Marshall Cavendish Corp, 2002, p. 460.
4. www.almaobservatory.org.
5. Serafin, Gianandrea, *L'interpretazione del crimine* [*The Interpretation of Crime*], Tangram, 2012, p. 93. The concept was first expressed by Emile Durkheim (1858–1917), as the cause of the phenomenon of anomie, a term that represents the rupture of the equilibrium within society following a crisis of values (see Sant'Ambrogio, A., Rosati, M. (ed.), *Emile Durkheim, Contributions for a Critical Re-reading*, Meltemi, 2002, p. 135).
6. Bonnet, Corinne, Scarpi, Paolo, *Religions Orientales – Mystic Cults: Neue Perspektiven – Nouvelles Perspectives – Prospettive nuove*, Verlag, 2006, p. 173.
7. Bertholet, Edouard, *La reincarnazione nel mondo antico* [*Reincarnation in the Ancient World*], Edizioni Mediterranee, 1994, p. 183.
8. Plato, Teeteto, 166 D = DK80 A 2 1.
9. Manodori Sagredo, Alberto, *Anfiteatri, circhi e stadi di Roma* [*Amphitheatres, Circuses and Stadiums of Rome*], Newton & Compton, 1982, p. 60.
10. Calvani, Vittoria, Giardina, Andrea, *Le vie della storia* [*The Paths of History*], vol. 2, Editori Laterza, 1979, 1986, pp. 52–58.
11. Jean-Jacques Rousseau, Benjamin Franklin, Voltaire, for example, embraced vegetarianism as an ethical choice of respect for nonhuman life. Rousseau devoted ample space to the theme in his *Èmile ou de l'education.*
12. If, on the one hand, the movement and activism in favor of nonhuman animals in recent years have been committed to affirming real rights, through the transposition by the laws in force, on the other hand, currents remain or are affirmed of thought that contest the effectiveness of legislative instruments. In particular, the so-called neo-welfare proposes, or at least supports, legislative reforms that are not based on the recognition of rights of nonhuman beings, but which in any case have them as their object: for example, the laws against maltreatment are widespread throughout the Western world and, although apparently protect nonhuman animals, the underlying ratio legis is the protection of the human feeling of pity toward them. There are also completely different positions, such as those of ecofeminism, which consider the right itself to be a patriarchal and hierarchical heritage that is unsuitable for recognizing the reasons of the individual, and which, therefore, contrast it with the individual concept of "ethics of relationships."
13. Bentham, Jeremy, *An Introduction to the Principles of Morals and Legislation*, J. H. Burns, H. L. A. Hart, Athlone Press, 1970, pp. 282–283.

14. Singer, Peter, *Animal Liberation*, 1975, Harper Perennial Modern Classics; Updated ed., 2009, p. 186.

15. Singer himself takes note of the above in describing his transition from omnivorous to "quasi-vegetarian," while he continued to eat the so-called seafood, only to be persuaded that, in doubt whether they feel pain, it is appropriate to abstain from it.

16. Kant, Immanuel, [1784–5] 1997: 212 [Ak 27: 459].

17. Western legal systems, in establishing rules for the protection of animals, not recognizing them as legal entities, and therefore not considering them capable of becoming holders of rights, have adopted the expedient of the so-called indirect duties, formally entitling these rules to the protection of the feeling of human piety. It is therefore defined as an indirect duty that duty addressed directly to human interests (capital, piety, etc.), and indirectly to animals, which represent the object of protection, but not the protected interest. A formulation based on "direct" duties would disregard the human interests involved and would presuppose the recognition of the ownership of rights in the animals themselves.

18. Regan, *The Case for Animal Rights*, University of California Press, 1983, p. 243.

19. Francione, *Animals as Persons: Essays on the Abolition of Animal Exploitation*, Columbia University Press, 2009, p. 106.

20. Francione, Ibidem, p. 51.

21. Ibidem, p. 15.

22. Ibidem, p. 12.

23. See, for example, the controversy related to the nature of viruses.

24. Ryder, R. D., *Victims of Science: The Use of Animals in Research*, London, Davis-Poynter, 1975.

25. https://link.springer.com/referenceworkentry/10.1007%2F978-3-642-11274-4_1128.

26. https://www.merriam-webster.com/dictionary/primordial%20soup.

27. Baker, Joanne, *50 Great Ideas you Really Need to Know*, Quercus, 2010, pp. 197–198.

28. Fenchel, Tom, *The Origin and Early Evolution of Life*, Oxford University Press, 2003, p. 12.

29. Naess, Arne, The Shallow and the Deep, Long-Range Ecology Movement: A Summary, in *The Deep Ecology Movement: an Introductory Anthology*, of Alan Drengson and Yuichi Inoue, Berkeley, North Atlantic Books, 1995. Find it here: http://www.ecology.ethz.ch/education/Readings_stuff/Naess_1973.pdf

30. Ibidem.

31. Ibidem.

32. https://www.britannica.com/topic/deep-ecology.

33. Huxley, Aldous, *Perennial Philosophy*, Harper & Brothers, 1945.

34. Metempsychosis, or metensomatosis, in Greek philosophy starts from Pythagoras, who, according to what is attested by tradition, would have been able to remember different lives. The concept of soul survival pervades many classical philosophers, including Empedocles and Plotinus, but, above all, Plato. He dedicates the myth of Er to the explanation of the phenomenon, which assumes fundamental

importance in the metaphysical conception of him: through reincarnation – explains Plato – the human being faces the catharsis that will lead him to return to the world of ideas, escaping the earthly experience.

35. http://www.eco-action.org/dt/thinking.html.

36. Although the proponents of ecosophy deny the concept of utility, it is evident that it reemerges and is the foundation of general consideration based on which the value of the individual is commensurate with his participation in a wider system. Belonging to a system of elements that are only apparently distinct, but in truth connected, is an evident fact and admitted by Eusebism, which nevertheless correlates it to the principle of respect and that of necessity.

37. Lanza, Robert, *A New Theory of the Universe*, The American Scholar, 2007.

38. Lanza, Robert, Berman, Bob, *Biocentrism: How Life and Consciousness are the Keys to Understanding the True Nature of the Universe*, Benbellabooks, Inc, 2009.

39. Ibidem, pp. 159–160.

40. Ibidem, p. 159.

Chapter 2

Beyond the Points of View – Eusebism

The history of philosophical thought shows that complex theories have often been formulated to justify preconceived ideas conceptually: in this way, it is impossible to arrive at universally valid definitions of principle.

Many claim that they do not seek the absolute and that thought is necessarily relative and subjective: this is not entirely exact, and, above all, it cannot exempt the thinker from dealing with the search for objective principles.

Identification is fundamental to find absolute principles. Therefore, after elaborating a theory, it is necessary to self-identify with everything other than oneself and ask oneself if that theory could be considered equally valid from all other viewpoints.

Everything comes from definitions: what is "other than oneself"? What is "alike"? Unfortunately, these are widely misunderstood concepts, often used (above all) by those who intend to face and overcome discrimination.

A humanist, in deprecating discrimination, would focus on gender, race, religion, etc., always focused on humans only.

An animal rights activist focuses his attention on the differences in species. Still, if he correctly begins to reject those between humans and mammals, he then begins to draw increasingly blurred boundaries as he moves toward more different animal life forms, up to the insects, which are also excluded from the philosophical animal rights theories.

A biocentrist extends the principle of "other" to consider everything that represents life, in any nature or form but ends up excluding one category, that is, nonlife.

Another underlying problem crosses humanism, animal advocacy, environmentalism/ecology, and biocentrism: all these currents of thought focus on specificity, extending or narrowing the recipients of their interest, but losing sight of the individual interactions within the same categories.

Establishing exact criteria for identifying discrimination does not automatically mean removing them, nor does it imply creating a complete philosophical system capable of exerting its effects in the context of everyday life, as well as in the long term. Although the formulation of the thesis may be positive, the underlying concepts are of a negative type: opposition to discrimination. Once it has been explained why discrimination is not morally acceptable, it is necessary to formulate organic models, which are not limited to the enunciation of nondiscriminatory alternatives, but also consider all the other aspects of existence to continue addressing it overcoming discriminatory conceptions. Bentham, overcoming the commonplaces of the time with his thought, had already sanctioned that animals should be included in the moral system based on the consideration that it does not matter if they speak, but only if they suffer.[1]

Thanks to this reflection, there is no doubt that it was also possible to include nonhumans in the balance of interests. Still, it is a partial inclusion, not already absolute, and always subjective. There would be a similarity between human and nonhuman suffering.

For the same reason, they maintain a subjective, and consequently wrong, perspective along with all the philosophical perspectives on animal rights that aim to underline the similarities and similarities between species: it is understood that the need for the observer is inherent in this operation. To find justificatory elements to refrain from carrying out dispositive acts against something other than oneself.

There are two methodological errors in this approach: the first is that asking the question "why should I respect it?" implicitly implies the consideration of oneself as arbitrators of who or what is other than oneself; the second error consists in the implicit emotionality when the similarity is attributed fundamental importance in theory philosophical.

There is a contradiction between the claim to reason philosophically (i.e., rationally) and the use of emotions and feelings.

On the other hand, if the reference to the ability to suffer was not intended as an expression of empathy, it is unclear why the logical path of affirming animal rights would always pass from confrontation with humans.

Eusebism seeks to overcome all the misunderstandings that have so far run into philosophical currents which, too focused on single aspects of life or single species, have lost sight of the overall vision and, above all, have been based on erroneous assumptions taken for granted, but which were only fruit of the observer's perspective.

Often the content of the ten commandments is used to show that they, containing typical precepts of the time, not universally valid and always could not have come from the divinity.

A similar argument can be made for all the philosophies of the past, which in the minds of their authors should have represented certain and lasting values, not only the ones applicable and limited to their time.

On the other hand, modern philosophies have become so specific and redundant that they close in on themselves and create systems of such complexity that they cannot be considered absolute but necessarily linked to the subject's ideas and the historical, social context of reference.

Eusebism intends to recover the linearity of ancient philosophies, aiming at simplifying thought, making it intelligible by all, and aspires to an absolute and not simply relative value.

How is this done?

First, it is necessary to reverse the perspective: we must not ask ourselves why to abstain from disposing of others, but the opposite: "Why would I have the right to dispose of others?"

It will also be necessary to disregard the reference to the human being as a touchstone and avoid that the scope of consideration of philosophy is only the result of an extension of the current one rather than an all-encompassing inclusion.

Once the above steps have been carried out correctly, one should not be able to say whether a stone or a human being theorized it.

The paradox is deliberate: we know very well that a stone cannot formulate philosophical theories, but this does not mean that it participates less than us in the Universe to which we belong and, indeed, certainly resisted even us and our ancestors and, thanks to it and to many other objects that we define inanimate, has made our birth possible.

Our knowledge is limited to physical and phenomenal reality, which is to say that it is severely limited. Therefore, we should modify our philosophical theories toward understanding the Universe and, therefore, science and technology.

The greatest aim that a philosophical theory can propose again is not to examine facts and notions of the past or already known, but to create a method capable of guaranteeing a correct approach to problems and circumstances that are still unknown and not occurred.

One of the main errors of modern philosophies is that of being fossilized on issues that are flawed at the outset, such as the existence or not of absolute principles: on the one hand, those who supported them, such as the deontologists, took sides, while on the other the relativists delighted in refuting one for such a thesis.

Eusebism is based on some essential principles, which aim to be valid at any juncture and from every perspective: from this fundamental and absolute core, it will then be possible and necessary to take into consideration the relative and subjective, which are part of existence, and which cannot be ignored.

2.1 THE PRINCIPLE OF RESPECT

Unconditional respect, pure and free from any prejudice, is the only correct way to relate to everything around us.

The Greek word εὐσέβεια was used to define a sense of respect of exceptional breadth, and this is what inspires the definition of the thought described in this work.

In the archaic meaning, the term designated the broadest feeling of respect in relationships with others, not just humans: in this way, the inner predisposition to welcome the other and recognize what was due was identified.

Acting according to *eusebeia* meant respecting one's duties, the other forms of life, and the divinities[2]; this word was also used to indicate the concept of dharma in the Greek translation of the Edicts of 250 BC of the Indian emperor Ashoka: conducts such as good faith, moderation, respect for every form of life, generosity and compassion can be ascribed to both definitions.[3]

Throughout history, the term *eusebeia* was increasingly identified with nuances linked to the relationship with the divinity, both in pagan and Christian cults, losing most of the nuances and breadth of the original meaning, which contained within itself the whole precept of living harmoniously and respectfully. However, today we can recover the original meaning of this old expression and define Eusebism as the current thought based on unconditional respect for anything.

The first precept of Eusebism is that it is not necessary to find a justification to recognize respect but—on the contrary—to deny it.

Eusebism owes its name to the recovery of the term's original meaning, extended to include respect for everything that exists. Thus, in the Eusebist meaning, the terms "other" or "neighbor" refer to everything that exists.

Of course, there is not a single form of respect universally applicable. Still, it is necessary to identify the characteristics of the other, in order, if necessary, to limit or modify the minimum quantity and quality of consideration to be recognized: it is not necessary to behave in the same way with a stone and with a human being but to respect both.

A moral system can be considered universal if it is valid for everything, including humans, animals, the environment, the Earth, and the solar system. Thus, for example, man freely polluted the Earth and the air and waters until the consequences became, for themselves, harmful and threatening.

Since space exploration began, the same mentality has caused pollution consisting of debris and wrecks that crowd the Earth's orbit or that have dispersed adrift in space regardless of the consequences, but are not in people's sphere of interests.

With the onset of the atomic age, we have threatened the Earth with destruction and, for now, the threat has been averted: it will probably recur in the future, with the shift of planetary balances to the east, but perhaps it will not be necessary to worry about a further evolution of science and technology or thought, at least not for some century or millennium.

On the other hand, even if human beings will be able to avoid a new Middle Ages, perhaps postatomic, this does not imply that their potential harmfulnes decreases. In contrast, when we can master quantum physics and manipulate the main forces, we will be able to create a black hole capable of swallowing entire solar systems or even galaxies, even during simple experiments.

Human history is full of improper uses of new scientific discoveries and inventions: just think of the X-rays used to shoot videos of curious and cheerful subjects, at least before discovering the tumors that such exposures had caused, or the small crowds of Italian children that offered themselves after World War II smiling at the cameras as US Army medical workers sprinkled them with DDT against parasites, before discovering that it too was carcinogenic; not to mention asbestos, considered the panacea for many constructions, from buildings to naval and still in use when its carcinogenicity had already become known.

The few examples above warn us to consider with the utmost respect not only sentient beings or living beings but all objects, since interfering with their nature means altering, sometimes even irremediably, equilibria that can hardly be understood.

Men are not obliged to pursue a certain type of progress; they can choose. The price of evolution can never be paid by those who do not have the right to choose; for this reason, neither experimentation on animals nor the actions capable of affecting the environment can be remitted to human will.

A moral focused on the principle of respect requires that each choice has to be oriented toward protecting and safeguarding the whole, avoiding behaviors that could damage something that surrounds us in the name of selfishness.

In short, we will have to consider the consequences (favorable and unfavorable) deriving from our actions concerning all those involved: no action can be considered just if it favors the agent's interests to the detriment of all others.

We can reach the same conclusion by assuming that we move from both an altruistic and selfish perspective: when acting in the interest of others, the purpose and the cause coincide. If, on the contrary, we started from a selfish perspective, the conclusions would be identical. If each of us operated in the interest of others automatically, our good would be pursued much more than the other way around since, in one case, we would be the only ones to pursue it against all the others. In contrast, in the second case, the proportion would be reversed.

We fight every day to assert our rights or our needs, trying not to be overwhelmed by others, striving to obtain our spaces by limiting those of others: we prefer to deprive our neighbor rather than ourselves, and we prefer to enrich ourselves more than our colleagues.

If it is true that human existence without impact is unthinkable, it is also true that it is necessary to refer to the Kantian distinction in terms of pure reason and practical reason: the first, pure moral, represents the ideal, while the second, related to living daily, is the necessary tool of human interactions.

If we can aspire not to damage anyone, then it must be acknowledged that this can be impossible or extremely demanding in material coexistence, so much so that it is even uncontrollable by society.

Pure morality and practical morality find a meeting point in the principle of altruism: while it is not often possible to know a priori what is good and how to achieve it, it is nevertheless fundamental to distinguish between the moral attitude of those who work to procure the good of others and those who, on the contrary, seek their own benefit only.

The principle of equilibrium is the only absolute and the only parameter universally suitable for determining the long-term functioning of any activity within a closed system. From economics to human relationships, any initiative that cannot apply this principle is doomed to failure. The only unknown factor may concern the time required for this to occur. Therefore, it is unnecessary to resort to the principles of altruism or solidarity to infer that the agent's interest and protection and that of the recipient of the action depend on the respect that one can apply to act. For the same reason, we must conclude that it is misleading to speak of conflicting interests since if what harms or benefits one also harms or benefits the other, then there are no more opposing interests but a single interest.

A practical demonstration of the above: overexploiting environmental resources to foster personal ambitions can, in the immediate future, bring a benefit to the agent and damage the recipient of the action, but in the long term, the agent will not only be unable to achieve his ambitions but will also have to strive to restore balance.

Should we assume that only humans or sentient beings can be rightsholders? If this were the case, each of us would automatically be entitled to dispose of, in full, everything that does not enjoy rights, which cannot be possible by definition: if a tree did not have rights, anyone could cut down an infinite number of trees, thus determining an unsustainable and, therefore, impossible situation.

As such, a universal right, which as such preexists man and even life itself (as it is conventionally understood today), should abandon any subjective perspective. This requires an absolute and abstract reflection that could appear so far from everyday activities as irrelevant, but it is not. Only by starting from such a principle, we can reach conclusions valid not only "here" and "now," but "always" and "everywhere."

OUT OF THE ORDINARY

One of the most common clichés is that respect presupposes acceptance or analogy (if not identity) between the person who recognizes it and the one to whom it is recognized. This mentality cannot be shared since it is not founded on objective circumstances, implying the subjectivization of morality.

It can be said that:

-if A enjoys the respect
and
-if B = A
then B enjoys the respect.

The above said represents a sufficient but unnecessary condition.

In the first place, if it were affirmed that the syllogism is a necessary condition, before being respectful of the neighbor, one should wait to have the certain proof of his identity with the other taken by comparison.

Furthermore, relating different entities to practice discrimination (between those who enjoy respect and those who do not) would imply the attribution of the quality of judge to the agent, who should be (or considered) superior to it.

Precisely for these reasons, there is a widespread misunderstanding that confuses the concept of respect with that of adhesion or sharing, underlying expressions such as: "white people and black people are the same," "the disabled," "even animals suffer."

All the above claims are antidiscriminatory, yet they bear the seed of discrimination inherent in the principle that respect is due only to equals.

Let us reason contraries: if it were proved that black people are not the same as white people, that the disabled are disabled, and that animals do not suffer, then it would be possible to conclude that they are inferior and therefore unworthy of our respect.

Eusebism opposes the principles "I respect whom I like" and "I respect whoever looks like me," instead stating "respect regardless of appreciation and similarity."

To respect others, there is no need to transform reality through sterile rhetoric: it is sufficient to modify the mentality with which we approach it.

The first step in the direction suggested by Eusebism is to accept diversity, both qualitative and quantitative, as an inevitable circumstance of existence.

Someone can be considered less intelligent, less likable, less skilled in some specific activity without discriminating against them or limiting their self-determination or existence.

The most significant change of perspective that the human being can make is considering the dissimilar as himself, ceasing to reason by analogies.

Many philosophers think that empathy is necessary to determine who is owed what. It is a form of anthropocentrism that lacks any philosophical background. Such theories look more like the systematization of preconceived ideas rather than the impartial elaboration of ideas.

It is useless and even harmful to demand coherence between every single thought and every single action since, in this way, we end up rejecting all theories that would imply behaviors that we are not willing to implement.

By simply accepting that the human being is inherently inconsistent, one could avoid ending up in those intellectual pitfalls that limit the formulation of theories to what their authors are willing to put into practice.

How many smokers would fight for a ban on smoking? How many of them would promote information campaigns to quit smoking? Yet in his heart, every smoker knows the harmfulness of that action: why then justify it intellectually, if not to appear inconsistent?

But since every human being, in addition to having their tastes and preferences, is limited, how could any of us believe that his thought is objectively right if it ends up justifying and endorsing all his behaviors without questioning any of them?

To get out of the cliché "I do it, so it is right," the conceptual distinction between what is and what should be is relevant, allowing us to distinguish between the world that exists and what should exist.

2.2 THE PRINCIPLE OF EQUILIBRIUM

Universalizing the concept of respect means emancipating it from the subjectivation of actions. In some cases, the implications of action are known and shared by the agent and the recipient of the conduct: if I punched a person passing by on the street, suddenly and without provocation, he would certainly be convinced that I was unrespectful and I would be equally aware of it. In this situation, it is easy to observe an objective and shared lack of respect. However, as the differences between the subjects affected by the action increase, uncertainty also increases: for a dog, being stroked on the belly represents a gesture of affection, while a cat can consider it aggression and feels entitled to react with violence.

There are interactions in which the concept of respect can become extremely labile; think, for example, of the ecosystem: it is extremely unlikely that human beings can experience empathy toward it or figure an interest proper to a tree, a forest, or even a rock. On the other hand, the principle of equilibrium acts as an objective reference, which allows to easily overcome any conflict in conjunction with the other principles of Eusebism. Therefore, in the example above, can it be considered "right" to pollute the environment since there would be no respect, as demonstrated by altering the balance that this determines?

The principle of equilibrium does not concern only infrahuman relationships or interspecies, but it can be applied indiscriminately to any interaction, even toward oneself. One of the most controversial issues is the lion and the gazelle, or, more generally, the "morality" of predators.

Predators exist as long as they have prey, and therefore rights (or the absence of them) cannot be given to one and the others. What acts as supreme authority and guarantor is the principle of equilibrium: the prey that eats vegetables is destined to suffer when it causes their disappearance, and the predator that hunts too much will perish after killing its last prey.

Equilibrium is based on very precise and easily verifiable rules. Although it certainly cannot be identified with the definition of "right" in the technical sense, it nevertheless imposes and demands the respect of necessary conducts. We can consider necessary the conducts that, if note respected, cause damage to the agent.

A definition of the "law" is: "A binding custom or practice of a community: a rule of conduct or action prescribed or formally recognized as binding or enforced by a controlling authority."[4]

The codification of laws in Western societies does not represent an alternative to cosmic ordering principles any more than the social norms sanctioned and respected by communities of primates, cats, or even insects. On the other hand, positive law is necessary for the coexistence of associates in any society, but, at the same time, it exclusively binds (or should bind) those who participate in it, sharing duties and rights: to affirm that only humans are capable of making law would mean ignoring that even within of an anthill there is a rigid order with precise rules of conduct, rights, duties, and sanctions.

No man would accept to be condemned for violating a law sanctioned in an anthill since he would most likely consider it extraneous to his system of values and experiences. The equilibrium can be considered under different aspects: first, it is a proportionate mutual interest satisfaction. Second, the principle of equilibrium can also be defined based on functional factors: the system within which all factors can perform their functions correctly is balanced.

Common to both definitions is that there is no need for external interventions to the system under consideration for its proper functioning: if everyone's interests are respected, then there is no need for laws nor a judicial system. Likewise, if all parts of a mechanism are working properly, no modifications or repairs are required.

Nothing prevents a legal system from renouncing to pursue equilibrium, but what consequences does it entail? First, it is necessary to make frequent investments of resources to keep the unbalanced system in operation since, as mentioned, it cannot sustain itself.

The less balanced are the interests of different parts of the population, the greater are social conflicts.

It is no coincidence that monarchy has survived only in the countries where it opened to popular demands.

Every behavior or thing that afflicts the equilibrium ends up being destroyed by the system to which it belongs, as in the Universe, is in our planet. If, for example, a species reproduces itself so much that it runs out of food resources, it ends up extinguishing itself, or at least drastically resizing itself, until it reaches the balance between the number of their specimens and the resources available again.

Based on the principle of equilibrium, it could not be said that saving an individual's life represents an absolute good. On the contrary, to the extent that this threatens the balance between the number of subjects and available resources, it can even be considered as an immoral action, no matter how much their existence determines the suffering or the disappearance of numerous other subjects.

In the case just described, the principle of equilibrium must also be related to noninterference and availability: to what extent is it permissible to interfere with what surrounds us? What, among what surrounds us, is left to our availability?

Is it correct to think that we can dispose of an entire species, as well as of the resources destined to (or usable by) it?

The principle of equilibrium is not only fundamental in the considerations concerning the environment or species, but it is also essential for governing relationships between individuals, be they business or emotional.

Just as between two business partners, balance can only work on the condition that both find similar interests. A couple is more close-knit the more similarities they share.

In human relationships, equilibrium can hardly be expressed through a mathematical formula. However, the satisfaction of interests in a broad sense can be configured even when there are no shared interests between the two members of a couple. Thus, for example, it may be that mutual expectations are met, thanks to the fact that one of the two is satisfied by being dominant and the other by being dominated; this is a balanced relationship, at least until the compatibility between mutual expectations fails. It is, instead, wrong to believe that the principle of equilibrium is satisfied only where all parties involved act in the same way.

Thus formulated, the principle of equilibrium must be parameterized from time to time to particular cases through empathy and objectification. We should not ask ourselves if a relationship is balanced based on what we believe the other should legitimately expect, but rather on what our partner actually expects.

2.3 THE PRINCIPLE OF NONINTERFERENCE

The principle of noninterference represents the natural expression of respect, in its pure and broadest sense: it would be erroneous to believe that it is possible to interfere only with beings endowed with self-determination since any atom, molecule, or particle enjoys intrinsic properties and possibilities that are unknown to us and often unpredictable.

Everything that exists can have an end, which can be self-referential or hetero-referential: a tree, for example, has numerous functions that make it useful not only to itself but to a multitude of other beings, from vegetable and animal kingdoms.

We should also admit that we cannot understand the purpose of everything around us.

To interfere means to modify or prohibit the purpose of someone or how that purpose is pursued.

Suppose we decide not to interfere only with those with purposes known to us and possibly shared. In that case, we would fall into the usual error of considering absolute truth what actually is a merely subjective point of view.

In a closed system, such as the Earth or the Universe, the same existence presupposes the interaction between different elements. Therefore, the principle of noninterference must be adapted from time to time. In this sense, we can consider the principle absolute, while the rules of conduct must be related and based on specific cases.

If we consider the relationship with other humans, the principle of noninterference can be formulated as follows: "Do not force the decisions of others."

In dealing with nonhuman animals, avoiding interference would mean refraining from any behavior that forces others to change their habits. A typical case is the removal of specimens from their habitat or the separation of groups.

Not knowing all the implications of our actions would be impossible to use absolute criteria and dictate rules valid for all situations. The only possible method is to recognize everything that surrounds us and to limit interference in principle and, when in doubt, if possible, to abstain.

In cases where it is impossible to refrain from behaviors that cause interference with what surrounds us, the conduct that causes the least interference (to our knowledge) is preferable.

The principle of noninterference implies deepening one's knowledge of oneself and the surrounding world and understanding each element's purpose and function within the system.

Not interfering means not damaging, limiting, or altering: we spend a lot of our time thinking about using things, people, and animals to achieve goals. Unfortunately, this attitude makes us lose sight of what is outside of us and prevents us from considering it according to its intrinsic value rather than as a mere tool to pursue selfish interests.

The fact of believing that someone or something exists only to serve us has provoked and continues to cause conflicts of all kinds, from the most trivial quarrels with those around us to wars on a world scale.

The search for constructive interactions, rather than destructive interference, represents one of the highest goals that we can set ourselves. To get closer to this ambitious goal, we must learn to overcome the limits of prejudice dictated by subjective points of view and start thinking about the whole picture in a 360-degree manner.

No one belongs to us, neither a child, nor an animal we have at home, nor the tree in the garden, nor the rocks of a mountain: with each of them, we can choose to relate as if we were masters or referees, or to use the principle of noninterference based on their specific skills and needs.

Mini-Interference

We cannot always adopt the principle of noninterference, especially in organized social relationships, which presuppose decisions with effects on many individuals: in all these cases, the criterion of mini-interference, that is, the minimum necessary interference, can help.

Using the mini-interference criterion, it is also possible to address the most frequent conflict situations, both in contingent reality and academic hypotheses, such as: "Is it right to sacrifice the individual for the multitude?"

According to the theory of individual rights, the answer would be negative since it is not conceivable to diminish the individual's rights, even in the face of the benefit of infinite others. On the other hand, biocentric theories, where they disregard the rights of individuals, would instead lead to a solution of the opposite type, considering the collective good more important than the individual one.

Even according to utilitarianism, the second solution would be the most moral, as the global level of well-being would increase (or decrease less). However, this simple example also shows one of the intrinsic limits and contradiction of utilitarianism: if it is true, as the founder of this current of thought already maintained that, "each counts one, no one counts more than one,"[5] then there would be no way to justify choices that would perfectly respond to the global assessment criterion of well-being.

Let us imagine that a nation, after decades of clashes between opposing factions, has found peace thanks to an enlightened leader and that one day this leader discovers that he has an incurable disease that could only be resolved through an organ transplant. In the event of the leader's death, the whole nation would suffer dramatic mourning. Moreover, it would risk plunging back into disorder and fratricidal clashes, with thousands of victims: in this perspective, choosing any individual and sacrificing their life to guarantee the leader the necessary organ for survival would represent an act in conformity with utilitarianism.

How is it possible, that each counts for only one if it is necessary to consider the overall welfare deriving from each action or omission?

The enlightened leader cannot count for one since the well-being connected with him is not only his. Therefore, he should count for as many as will be afflicted by his disappearance.

In short, by adopting the moral evaluation parameters of utilitarianism, there would be no room for absolute determination of the value of individuals, since each would have a different relevance depending on its relationship with the society: such criterion, at an "instinctive" level, is well summarized by the heartfelt plea that the designated victim punctually addresses to his or her executioner in dramatic films, asking to be spared since that murder would deprive the children of their parent.

The principle of mini-interference does not allow commissive interference, but only omissive: it is not permissible to interfere with the existence of others by harming, but only by helping.

If, for example, it was necessary to decide to whom, among several subjects, to allocate aid, it would be legitimate to choose the one whose asset has the greatest value for the system to which it belongs.

Eusebism builds a bridge between the theories of individual rights and biocentrism; this is possible using the principle of mini-interference, which, while recognizing the relativity of the value of each element based on the context, does not allow the individual to be diminished to the point of enslaving him to higher purposes.

If a common tree were cut down to plant a rarer one, applying the principle of noninterference would prevent this from being done. In contrast, the principle of mini-interference would allow exercising choice between several individuals in need of care, not available to everyone, based on their relevance to the context of belonging.

In short, it is not morally wrong to attribute a relative value to what surrounds us if this "evaluation" does not imply exploitation or undue interference.

2.4 THE PRINCIPLE OF CIRCULARITY

The principle of circularity is based on the repercussions of actions within a closed system. To virtuous actions correspond equally virtuous reactions. In contrast, negative reactions would result from malicious actions.

Inflicting evil on others is only apparently a one-way action since the harmful consequences could be amplified at the end of the circle, and they will also afflict the agent.

Although the following is abstractly referable to the entire Universe, for the sake of exposition and conceptual convenience, we will limit our field of speculation only to planet Earth and its inhabitants: we can think of this system as a circle, each of its elements as a dot. If each element omitted to make any exchange (both additive and subtractive) with the others, the circle would not be perfected, remaining only in appearance. At the same time, it would be possible to notice that the arrangement of the elements follows the trend of a circle, but without realizing it (figure 2.1).

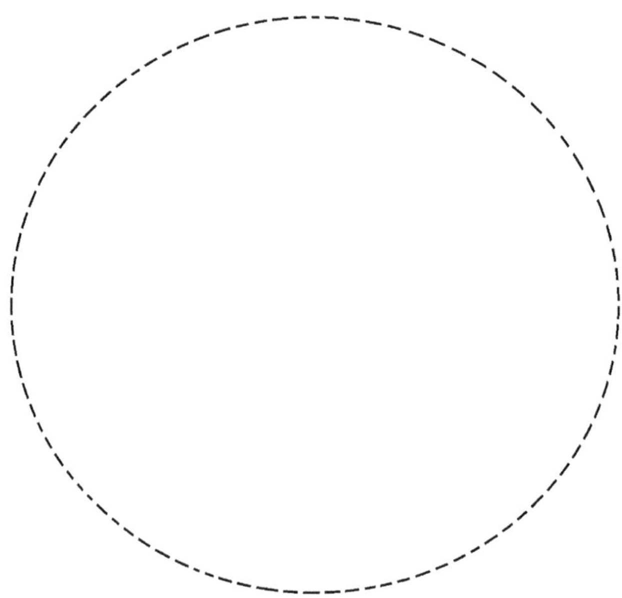

Figure 2.1. Isolated Individuals. *Source: Created by Author.*

If each element interacted with the others only in a subtractive way, receiving from the element that precedes it, but without returning to these or the next, the circle would not complete itself, resulting in a series of discontinuities (figure 2.2).

On the contrary, the perfect circle will be realized only when each element (point) achieves the correct balance based on the equivalence of giving and receiving (figure 2.3).

Therefore, the Earth system cannot be conceived based exclusively on the point of view of one of its components, whether it be humans, animals, or the environment: the correct perception can only mature by considering the influence of each element on all others.

At this point, it is not possible to say that only one element has rights without bestowing those rights to the other elements.

Of course, the altruistic principle by itself could produce substantial harmful effects, even worse than those caused by acting for selfish purposes. Human history is full of harassment, persecution, and prevarication perpetrated in the name of what some thought was right for others. For this reason, the principles of balance and noninterference must always be at the basis of practical moral.

From a strictly physical point of view, the concept of circularity finds expression in the first law of thermodynamics. Energy in an isolated system of forces is not created or destroyed but is transformed.[6] In chemistry,

Figure 2.2. One-way Exchange. *Source: Created by Author.*

Figure 2.3. Full Exchange. *Source: Created by Author.*

Lavoisier's law states that "nothing is created, nothing is destroyed, everything is transformed."[7]

Well before the modern sciences, classical philosophers "predicted" the concepts of circularity: in particular, the pluralist thinkers Empedocles, Anaxagoras, and Democritus theorized the existence of multiple principles of nature, from whose combination would derive variability of the states of existence, including how we define life and death.

The connection between everything that exists at a strictly material level is evident: distinguishing entities based on specificities is necessary. To believe that these can justify discrimination would be a contradiction in terms. Similarly, it is impossible to imagine a universe in which the actions of one on the other and vice versa are ineffective, based on some hierarchical principle.

NOTES

1. See above, note 17.
2. Charles, Jay Daryl, *The Unformed Conscience of Evangelism: Recovering the Church's Moral Vision*, Intervarsity Press, 2002, p. 168.
3. Singh, U., *A History of Ancient and Medieval India: From the Stone Age to the 12th Century*, Prentice Hall, 2009, p. 354.

4. https://www.merriam-webster.com/dictionary/law.

5. Bentham, Jeremy, *Rationale of Judicial Evidence*, 1827.

6. From a mathematical point of view, the first law of thermodynamics is expressed as follows: given two states, respectively state A and state B, the internal energy variation, represented by the equation $\Delta U = U (B) - U (A)$, is equal to the difference between the absorbed heat – represented as $Q = Q (A \rightarrow B)$ – and the work done by the system during the transformation – which can be represented as $W = W (A \rightarrow B)$, from which we get that $\Delta U = Q - W$.

7. Lavoisier, Antoine, *Traité Élémentaire de Chimie*, 1789.

Chapter 3

Right and Rights

3.1 BASIS

Rights are very curious things, as they are called into question by numerous disciplines, each of which approaches them from different perspectives.

This overlapping of perspectives has produced and continues to produce so many arguments that it would be impossible to account for them in a single work. Fortunately, this is not the purpose of my work.

On the other hand, rights, at whatever level they are understood, are an indissoluble element of any community. They can be understood in one way rather than another, accepted as a beacon of civilization, or even rejected, but they certainly cannot be ignored.

Before entering the merits of the vision of rights in Eusebism, it is necessary to dwell on some preliminary issues, starting with the relationship with other currents of thought.

I disagree with legal positivism, but, at the same time, I think that even criticizing it would be irrelevant and misleading, leading the reader to the persuasion that there is something to discuss.

The mere fact that a thought has arisen in a given historical period and that, subsequently and for various reasons, some thinkers have sustained it does not mean that such a thought is well-founded; therefore, scrambling around it would represent a useless and harmful endorsement.

Moreover, the hypothesis of legal positivism, which we could simplify in "What I call law is law," does not represent a theory at all, but the mere description of a fact, which would be similar to the statement that "Jack is the one who was called Jack by his parents."

This law theory can represent a useful tool in applying the rules by describing the operating principles and providing indices (efficiency, effectiveness, etc.). However, the statement on the origin of the law is completely tautological and therefore irrelevant.

Many have questioned and continue to wonder about the origin of law. There are plenty of philosophical theories about it: some take into account the law of nature, some the social contract, the international consensus, and even some that deny the need for law.

The Law of Nature

Philosophers said everything (and the opposite) about the law of nature. In the course of history, they have changed from affirming it to denying it, up to today's literal making fun of those who still claim its validity. In the interpretation of its supporters, the law of nature would represent an absolute principle preexisting to man, standardizing the entire existence on Earth and, therefore, not a human gimmick, but rather something that human beings can only recognize and, if anything, codify it. According to this thought, a positive law should be inspired by the rules of behavior innate in each of us and does not represent an abstract and creative activity but a mere recognition of something that preexists.

The concept of *lex naturalis* was already present in ancient Greece and Roman culture.[1]

Kant maintained that there was only one right based on the law of nature: freedom.[2]

Among the numerous contrary arguments, some are more recurrent: to name an illustrious one, Norberto Bobbio used the example of hereditary succession and the interpretative diatribes that it determined even within the natural lawyers themselves, opposing them in formulating different hypotheses about the most compliant "to nature" method to regulate this institute.

According to Bobbio, the simple existence of different theses on a topic (e.g., succession) would have shown the nonexistence of a single law of nature.

Bobbio's analysis seems simplistic, which is an obvious symptom of the widespread problem mentioned above: thinkers often do not approach the issues without prejudice but formulate thoughts to substantiate their beliefs.

Why, then, would Bobbio have been so superficial in his analysis?

Meanwhile, assuming that a current of thought is radically erroneous only because there is a disagreement between some of its exponents does not represent proof of any kind: it would be like saying that since physicists have different theories on the laws that govern nature, there are no physical laws. In short, the mere fact that not everyone knows a circumstance or can interpret it correctly does not mean that it does not exist or does not have a certain interpretation.

Another simplism is that we cannot expect to see all human beings' legal institutions reflected in nature.

Bobbio had presented the hypothesis of succession, but we could think of a road accident or compensation for damages. Is there in nature any principle for which those who have caused damage because of negligence must compensate it? In nature, perhaps, the concept of revenge may exist, but certainly not that of monetary compensation, since money does not exist in nature either. At most, one could think of the sense of "debt" in that those who have wronged others can be punished.

In the example analyzed by Bobbio, there is also a third misunderstanding, which concerns the concept of property: property, in nature, does not exist. Since everything is transformed, including animal life (therefore also human), one cannot think it is "natural" to have something before birth or after death.

An animal or a community uses the goods at its disposal to the extent that it can maintain control, which presupposes the strength and the will to oppose the attempts of others to take control.

Property is a concept that does not exist outside of human legal institutions. Therefore, discussing it based on any *lex naturalis* represents a mere exercise in rhetoric.

The fact that nature is based on certain rules is unobjectionable: if anything, we can only discuss what they are, not whether they exist.

The laws of chemistry and physics show how all nature is governed by imperative norms, which at the same time establish and delimit it since, without them, it would not exist, at least not in the way we know.

If animals did not kill each other, there would be an immense growth that would lead to the exhaustion of environmental resources and, therefore, of entire species or even of all life on Earth.

As noted by Kant, it is undoubtedly true that freedom represents a law of an absolute and omnipresent nature but ranging from the dimension of an individual law to the guiding principles of the whole, equilibrium is what the entire evolutionary process turns toward.

Although labels and the schematic framing of thought are some of the worst disasters of human existence, Eusebism does not reject the concept of the law of nature; however, we should avoid all attempts to relate abstract legal institutions created by the human being to the *lex naturalis*.

Eusebism accepts a sort of "minimal natural law," meaning to limit itself by taking note of those objective (and not presumptive) phenomena that occur in nature and allowing it to continue.

From the perspective of a minimal natural law, we can conclude that what contributes to evolution is right, and that, therefore, helps to balance opposite interests.

If it is true that nature rests on equilibrium, it is also true that altering or decreasing it causes damage to all members of the system (in this case, the terrestrial) and that it is therefore certainly wrong.

The Social Contract

Contractualism is an important theory on the source of power, which produces a law. It was formulated for the first time by John Rawls in *A Theory of Justice*.[3] According to his thesis, all community members agree to submit to mutual limitations (duties) while affirming legitimate claims (rights). In this theory, the community members would consent to found positive laws, which are the laws of a civil society, while not excluding the laws of nature in this process, which by some contracts are still considered the inspiration.

The most extreme positions of contractualism affirm that "right" would be what the will of the society expresses, and, therefore, any rule of law widely approved would be considered right, regardless of whether it can be ascribed to natural principles or not.

There is a connection between natural laws and contractualism, which some consider as an emanation: those who share this approach recognize the presence of natural laws, which they consider the ideal goal of right and laws.

John Rawls gave an important impetus to this doctrine. He underlined the importance of the distinction between the concept of "good" and "just," observing that the latter must prevail over the former to avoid leading to anything arbitrary.

From a philosophical perspective, contractualism is little more than a description of what the simple observation of the world makes evident: since the laws exist, individuals submit to them demanding the same from other affiliates.

From a juridical point of view, in my opinion, the theory shows evident limits when it refers to individuals unable to express a will, such as infants, people with mental disorders, and such: for all of them, the same laws apply, and even if it is true that these may enjoy specific exceptions, the duties of other individuals toward them do not cease, despite the lack of correspondence and the manifestation of will.

Regardless of the "marginal" cases (which are not so marginal, necessarily concerning all of us, at least for the first years of life), juridically speaking, one could also doubt the faculty of choice that is presented to a new member of a community: could he perhaps decide not to respect the laws, simply renouncing to be protected? No. What pact can exist when one of the contracting parties is forced to accept conditions preestablished by others?

In this sense, any mandatory rule represents the exercise of arbitration, as no negotiation is allowed about its content, and it does not presuppose any acceptance.

The main limitation of contractualism, in my opinion, is in the universality of positive law: it is not applied exclusively to members of a community but also to anyone else who falls within its sphere of competence (usually based on territory).

Did the slaves ask to be taken to foreign lands or to adhere to their laws? No, yet this has never precluded the applicability of those rules to them.

Rawls himself unwittingly showed the limit of the contractualist theory, affirming that animals would be unable to stipulate the social contract. Therefore, humans would have no moral duty toward them.[4]

If what Rawls argues in contractualism were true, then the reverse should also be true: human beings cannot consider nonhuman animals within their laws.

It does not seem consistent to state that rights are based on consent and, at the same time, making laws that affect different species, which cannot express any inclination toward our laws.

Rawls' conclusion is contradictory, since if it is true that nonhumans cannot be active subjects in the social pact, then they cannot even be passive subjects: they must be completely extraneous to our legal system. The same considerations are valid about the environment since it is considered a mere tool; although it cannot express any will or self-determination, it is used by human beings at their sole discretion.

In this case, contractualism also fails, since performing operative acts on the environment means automatically interfering with others, human and nonhuman, limiting their prospects of life or realization, and, in any case, precluding access to those same resources or others connected.

Supporting contractualism also implies accepting as absolute truth what is instead a simple presumption, that is, that only the human community is endowed with a system of rules. At the same time, science has shown that this is not correct.

If it is tautological to say that only human beings possess a right in the technical sense (after all, how could this not be the case, since we are the architects of this definition and category?), it is now evident that within every community animal rules of conduct are in force, the violation of which determines sanctions, the worst of which is the removal from the group.[5]

It is somehow ironic to observe that the pure contractual theory is probably applied in full among nonhuman animals: none of them is forced to adhere to the obligations of behavior accepted by others and, if they decide not to do so, they can simply move away from the collective.

In this different perspective, which considers not only the sense of justice and human norms but also that of all other animals, the most spontaneous conclusion is that each group should limit the sphere of application of the rules to its members and to those who, even if they are not part of it, can enjoy both duties and rights.

Utilitarianism

Although its roots go back to ancient Greece, one of the most recent moral theories is utilitarianism, which has arisen with Jeremy Bentham and is now supported by many scholars.

The fundamental postulate of utilitarianism is that the good coincides with the right: the law should maximize well-being as the final goal.

The formulation is generic, so much so that it has given rise to the most disparate interpretations: what is good? Who are the subjects whose good must be taken into consideration? How should it be measured?

Utilitarianism has been accused of accentuating individualism, but this is not necessarily true. Indeed, the opposite tends to be true: considering that the greater quantity of happiness coincides with the juster, it should be concluded that the individual disappears before collective interests.

On the other hand, other criticisms are far more relevant, highlighting that the vanishing of "happiness" cannot be considered unfounded. In the first place, philosophy has always questioned the meaning of this expression, sometimes reaching opposite conclusions or even renouncing any conclusion.

Even if we agree about what happiness is, we must take into account people's subjectivity. Everyone has a different idea of well-being and the methods to achieve it, so much so that it would be impossible to provide a single rule that is always valid.

Richard B. Brandt tried to overcome the latest criticism by linking the rules of conduct to psychology, to sanction precepts whose validity derives from the intrinsic value of the action; in his theory, not all individual aspirations deserve to be taken into consideration, but only those whose formulation would not change if the individual carried out psychological therapy.[6]

Brandt's attempt stems from the false (or, at least, arbitrary) assumption that psychology is a certain, exact, and objective science: this is not the case; therefore, it is impossible to seek an absolute evaluation from a relative system.

Above all, from the point of view of the law, Brandt's utilitarianism represents an illusion since the codification of a legal system based on such presuppositions would be completely arbitrary and would produce far from desirable effects, especially as antithetical to the principle of identification advocated by Hare.

One of the most important intuitions of utilitarianism, made by R. M. Hare, matches the commandment, "Do unto others as you would have others do unto you." The principle of identification is to be placed at the foundation of morally oriented actions to establish whether they can be just.

A rule based on the quantity of well-being deriving from every single action must be based on a case-by-case adaptation, and this would be something completely relative: this makes utilitarianism the opposi of Kantian deontology, for which the need to stand as an absolute beacon of morality.

But how can the well-being of others be increased without knowing what it consists of?

And, on the other hand, how can we determine what happiness represents for those other than us with absolute certainty?

All the corrections made throughout the history to the original principle have shown at least two things: (i) that principle can be considered as a "framework norm," indicating at most the end but not the means to pursue it; (ii) corrective measures are also affected by the same uncertainty and subjectivity of the underlying principle.

In my opinion, the fundamental criticism of utilitarianism is that it can be used to justify any potential harassment since it opens the door to the hypothesis that "the end justifies the means": it is a fundamental flaw underlying the whole doctrine, which can only be partially mitigated using all those complementary criteria that some utilitarians have suggested.

Is utilitarianism, therefore, to be rejected at all? Despite the numerous criticisms, I do not think so: the concept that happiness represents a fundamental parameter of morally oriented acting must be considered.

Precisely because living beings, by their very nature, have different approaches toward existence, when one considers the "social" activities and the interactions with others, the concept of what is "right" may differ from that of what causes other people's happiness.

Utilitarianism fills some gaps in deontology, which in its search for the absolute is destined to be shipwrecked against the relativity of life.

Take, for example, the question of whether lying is morally right or not: a deontologist's answer should be "yes" or "no," while a utilitarian's answer would be "it depends."

Is it more right (or better) to lie not to cause the unhappiness of others but simultaneously to compromise one's conscience, or the opposite? In this case, utilitarianism can provide a rule that takes into account the specificities.

On the other hand, what is the value of one's alleged moral integrity if the price is the unhappiness of others?

It would be difficult to imagine an ideal world in which everyone maintains their moral integrity to the detriment of the happiness of others. At the same time, a world in which everyone works for the happiness of others would certainly be more empathic, friendly, and harmonious.

The Foundation of Rights in Eusebism

A common mistake is to adhere to a doctrine, as this implies two mistakes: the first, accepting all its principles uncritically, and the second, rejecting the other theories a priori.

In a world dominated by relativity, the contamination of ideas is also a value.

What is the point of saying that a community of lions does not have the same laws or codes as humans? This is not a discovery but a piece of evidence.

Similarly, how can it be said that a driving rule represents a transposition of the natural order in attributing prevalence to lights over horizontal signs?

We should note that the only law that can be abstractly referable to principles of nature is criminal law. At the same time, the attempts to bring back civil and administrative rules are doomed to fail due to the inconsistency of the presuppositions: if anything, the latter should be inspired by utilitarianism as, not being possible to seek a sense of absolute justice, only global satisfaction could legitimize the action of the legislator.

Should we conclude that only humans can figure the right? They create their rights, and their laws descend from this, but it does not imply that the idea of moral right and evil cannot exist out of human societies.

What should be, however, is a criminal law inspired by absolute and not relative moral principles, as it happens instead: the first demonstration of the subjectivity of human rights is that it does not protect the just for the just, but it protects the interests of those who create it.

If absolute principles inspired the law, there would not be the need for continuous adjustments of principles that, instead, have always occurred in human history. There would be no need to abolish discriminatory norms simply because they would never have been formulated.

The fundamental problem that has never been overcome is the subjectivity of the legislator: the whole history of human rights is a succession of extensions of protected interests. At the same time, minorities or the weak or marginalized are forced into an eternal struggle to achieve the institutionalization of their interests through legislative transposition.

The criminal law must be inspired by the principle of equilibrium, which is a principle present and regulating any phenomenon in the world.

Considering a criminal law separate from any natural law means admitting any arbitrariness, since—like utilitarianism—it would be up to the legislator to decide, from time to time, what is right and what is wrong.

This way of thinking has given humanity a poisoned fruit, that is, a world torn apart by wars and discrimination, increasingly at risk of self-destruction and dominated by individualism: these are the consequences of the principle

"I am free to do what I want," applied on a large scale, which is reflected in legal positivism.

At this point, it is necessary to define what is right in a nontechnical sense: this can be considered a legitimate expectation of individuals toward others. This is something that happens not only in human societies.

At the most elementary level (without artifacts, interpretations, or codifications), right is part of individuals' personalities: anyone has different expectations toward others and reacts in different manners when such expectations are disregarded.

When several individuals share expectations, these become rules of conduct, and their violations imply sanctions. Sanctions are not only (and not necessarily) inflicted by the injured party but also by the other members of the community: this is the basic institutionalization of the law, but it is not exclusively human.

Bekoff and Pierce, in their Wild Justice,[7] have extensively examined the behavior of nonhuman animals, starting from the concept of justice as a "set of expectations about what one is worthy to receive and how one should be treated."[8] Their thesis is that the idea of justice is innate in man. It manifests one evolutionary continuity that would make it impossible to exclude nonhumans.

The authors underline that a clue to the fact that the sense of justice is not acquired can be seen in the behavior of children, whom just a few months old can show this characteristic, for example, by preferring the characters who play the role of the "good ones" in a puppet show.[9]

Even Hare, in his utilitarianism of the two levels, had acknowledged that the awareness of what is right is innate in the human being.[10]

If the sense of justice is innate, then it cannot be the exclusive prerogative of the human species, even if it can differ in quantity between one species and another.

Our species did not invent justice but limit itself to interpretation, just like all other animals and nature.

According to one of the most basic affirmations of human rights, "all men have the right to life," but if this were a right conceived and created by the community, then it would make no sense to speak of inalienability, as the very society that established it could at any time decide to revoke it. No one could affirm its universal nature, which is limited to the rule of the State in which it is in force.

In short, the legislator affirms at the same time two opposing and irreconcilable principles:

1) Everyone has inherent rights.
2) Only those designated by him have innate rights.

The observer, simply in the act of defining "who" is the holder of preestablished rights, arbitrarily excludes someone, which is objectionable, as it is done so by their definition and in contrast to the first principle.

Until recently, even in the Western world, it has always been taken for granted that the intrinsic difference between individuals of the human species was sufficient to justify different treatments, even normative ones: truly "universal" rights have never been affirmed in any legal system since historically only the concept of universality has changed, operating a continuous extension of the categories included; this, however, remains far from identifying the true literal meaning of the expression "universal."

Only what encompasses everything can be defined as universal. For this reason, only the recognition of rights, or, at least, of absolute obligations of conduct, toward everything that exists is universal.

Any attempt to make distinctions, based on any parameter devised by the observer, represents undue contamination: the extension of the sphere of rights based on human cultural and intellectual progress will always be in step with it, but it will inextricably depend on it.

The only solution to untie the conclusions from the observer's prejudices is to adopt a perspective independent from any evaluation, even the most elementary ones. Evaluations aimed at making distinctions are forms of prejudice, even those aimed at (and limited to) animal rights.

3.2 SUBJECTS VERSUS OBJECTS

The Prerequisites for the Ownership of Rights in the Human Society

Before establishing who the rightsholders are, it is necessary to ascertain the subjective prerequisite for their ownership based on what can be discriminated between who possesses these requisites and who does not.

Starting from the assumption that only human beings can be considered subjects of rights, we could figure, as we already have several times in science fiction literature,[11] the creation of an android, that is a synthetic version of a living being, endowed with self-determination, therefore able to understand himself and the surrounding world and to evolve, expressing preferences, choices, and opinions. If the android has human cognitive and analytical skills, the only difference would be that it was created in a laboratory and based on silicon instead of carbon. Such a being would be sentient, and it would have aspirations, being capable of suffering and evolving.

Could we define our android as a rightsholder, or should we consider it a simple object and, as such, not liable to become the owner of any type of right, nor, conversely, subject to any duty?

Before examining the favorable position, let us analyze the main reasons why it would be possible to deny rights:

i) It belongs to its creator.
ii) It does not have a soul.
iii) It is not natural.

The first argument was considered correct by many human societies, including Romans: the *pater familias*, holder of the *patria potestas* over his descendants, could dispose of life and death. Even beyond the laws in force, that right was compressed based on customs and habits, as well as a result of the social control exercised by relatives and neighbors: today, no Western state gives parents the right of life and death when it comes to their children, while, conversely, it imposes numerous duties and obligations on them.

The underlying principle is that having generated someone does not authorize them to dispose of them arbitrarily, but, on the contrary, it determines a responsibility on the person giving birth: think, for example, of the obligations of custody, maintenance, education, and even civil liability and criminality of the actions of the minor.

In today's Western thought, there is no argument of principle capable of justifying the free availability of an individual by another based on the causal link between the existence of the former and the will or conduct of the latter.

The inventor or creator enjoys rights limited to a period, after which they become collective patrimony; such limitation in time does not reflect any natural right of creation.

The second argument, namely the absence of a soul, raises at least two questions: what the soul is and whether only beings who have one can be rightsholders.

Currently, in the official culture, there is no certain data regarding the soul: religions, philosophies, and even science have been dealing with it for millennia, but—nevertheless—the state of the art of current human knowledge does not allow to identify the soul, if not by hypothesis and not without approximation; on the other hand, many even deny that it exists, while others argue that (in some form) it permeates everything, be it animate or inanimate.

Theories about the soul's diffusion in people evolved in step with human culture. This path can be considered an—at least partial—involution: from the belief that a common and transcendent essence pervaded everything, we reached the anthropocentric medieval Christian thought, which, codifying the concept of soul, attributed it exclusively to the human being.

Yet in the Age of Enlightenment, contemporary animal advocate philosophies, and, to a certain extent, even the church, have once again extended the number of possessors of a soul, to include at least nonhuman animals, who were previously excluded.

On the other hand, it is unclear where the soul resides, or what requisites an individual must possess to be endowed with it: for example, why should an android with memory, cognitive and analytical faculties, capable of understanding and willing, speaking and self-determination, be soulless?

According to some, a body designed in a laboratory and built artificially would host an energetic principle (soul).[12] If this were the case, it would be clear that the natural/artificial distinction would be unusable in examining the origin of the law in correlation with the existence of a soul.

But, even if science proves the absence of a soul in the android, it is not clear why only gifted subjects could be considered rightsholders: in this case, even human beings could not be eligible as rightsholders if they do not have a soul.

Who supports the equation "soul = rights" starts from the assumption that all human beings have a soul; it is a vicious circle since man professes its exclusivity even in the absence of certainties about the nature and diffusion of the soul builds entire moral systems on it.

The distinction between who is subject to rights and who is not cannot be based on something uncertain, since in this case, it would not have absolute value. Even if there were no doubts about "what" and "where" the soul is, would it be legitimate to argue that those without it have no rights?

The last critical argument, that the robot is not natural, as it is the result of human activities: based on that, also cloned human (or animal) beings are not the result of nature, but an artifice, and therefore they should not be eligible as rightsholders.

For many years medical science, also thanks to information technology, has been studying and manufacturing prostheses and even artificial organs, able to reproduce and replace damaged or sick human ones: we could therefore ask whether a man with an artificial arm or heart is yet to be considered a subject of rights.

Let us imagine a future (distant but not too far) in which most or all human organs, including the brain, are reproducible through biomechanical surrogates: an individual born in flesh and blood has slowly replaced all his organs with synthetic ones. Could they still be considered natural and, therefore, a rightsholder from this perspective?

In this regard, by going back to the question of the soul, we could ask ourselves where it lodges, and, therefore, to what extent or to what percentage of subrogation a man could go without losing it: perhaps if he had an artificial heart, this would cease to pervade him? Perhaps this would happen by replacing the brain or a certain percentage of organic/original/natural matter with an artificially produced and surgically implanted counterpart.

Those who believe in a god claim rights for themselves while admitting a higher creative and ordering authority. Referring to the android example, the question would be the same, with only two differences: (i) the creator would not be attributed divine characteristics, and (ii) the creation would not have organic nature (although even this latter presumption is not absolute).

If, for example, in a future—near or distant—man learns to animate matter, an individual still based on carbon (therefore organic) and made through a literal assembly of different parts—a sort of new Frankenstein—should be considered natural or artificial? Rightsholder or not?

Let us imagine that they are not endowed with self-determination, or, in transcendental terms, with a soul: having a shape and composition like ours, would they be rightsholders?

It is hard to see how it can be denied that an artificial, mechanical, and inorganic being, but endowed with self-determination, can enjoy rights, and, on the other hand, that an organic being does not enjoy them but is designed and "constructed" in a similar way, possibly even devoid of self-awareness or soul.

This speculation, which might appear sterile academic, has two specific purposes:

i) To demonstrate that philosophical reflection must relate to any context, present or future, real or hypothetical, to define universal and nonintended contents for the use and consumption of historical, political, and cultural contexts.
ii) To demonstrate that any a priori categorization aimed at including or excluding the existence of rights is erroneous, as it is based on limited knowledge and will be overcome with mental and scientific progress.

Subjects of Law and Objects of Rights

Contractualism is the theory of law that subordinated the ownership of rights to the individual's will more than any other did. Still, this manifestation of will is not only unnecessary but not even possible: every newborn, immigrant or incapable, is required to respect the laws of the state, whether it shares them or not, whether it invokes their protection or not.

Therefore, can it be excluded that the rightsholders can only stipulate the so-called social contract? The marginal cases are excluded as they are not significant and the "fewer marginals," as in the case of newborns, referring to their expectations, can undoubtedly be affirmed that "in nature" each community produces rules that can be kept in force only through shared acceptance and that presuppose awareness on the part of each: a lion in a community of lions learns the rules that govern it, while a wolf could not live in that community respecting its rules, since it is educated based on other, different ones that govern the packs of wolves.

At this point, a clarification is necessary: we will never see a lion sanctioning a wolf for not respecting the rules (laws) of the feline community.

In short, if a herd of lions adheres to certain rules, we do not expect others outside the herd to do the same: the rules of conduct are specific for each species and each group.

Many ask themselves: is it possible to recognize rights to entities other than humans within the so-called human rights? And if so, who—besides humans—can be the rightsholders? The question is misleading and badly posed: in this way, it is attributed to being a human faculty that does not belong to him, and that does not belong to the right that he created, that is, to be the supreme judge of all that surrounds him.

Human rights are not the only source of rights/duties, nor sanctions: it is only one of the countless sources that govern the living communities.

Each animal, within its species or group, participates in a system of obligations and expectations, regardless of any human legislator; therefore, the answer to the question, "Who is a rightsholder?" is: "All animals living in a community."

As for the human approach, the correct question to ask should be: "Who cannot be considered rightsholders?"

The difference between the two questions is not only formal but substantial: the first implies that anything to which rights are not explicitly recognized lacks them, while the second overturn the perspective, implicitly affirming that it is necessary to establish and prove the absence of rights and that, in the absence of such proof, one is supposed to be rightsholders. Until proven otherwise.

The superimposition of one order—in particular, the human one—to others is undue and wrong: it is based on anthropocentrism that leads us to consider the human being as a judge of all that exists.

A society that understood how adherence to the rules presupposes participation and "feeling" of the same cannot make the mistake of extending its precepts to those typically devoid of such prerogatives.

Does a wolf wonder if his puppy must be included in the rules of his community?

The presumption that the legislator's work conferred justification to undue dispositions has always prevailed in human history and has allowed discriminating sex, race, faith, and such.

Respect for the freedom and self-determination of others is the only true precept of nature that the philosophy of law can contemplate, being understood that the limit is always reciprocity.

The ideal of any legal system should be the exclusive discipline of its affiliates and the estrangement from any different body or subject: having ascertained that each of them is governed by its own rules, the attempt to counteract others would represent a completely arbitrary and unjustified act.

Let us think the other way around: if a community of wolves decided that human beings do not deserve rights, would this change, in theory, or substance, our lives and the way we perceive ourselves or pose ourselves?

The only real difference between the group of wolves and us, in interspecies relations, is that our cultural background is prodromal to the imposition of our choices and our dispositive acts on those who, in practice, can be subjugated.

Rome did not accept the laws of foreign nations but did not hesitate to bring its laws to those lands after having conquered them: today, just as then, we are willing to recognize rights only to those who have the strength to impose them. But this is not the logic of the law; it is the opposite! This is not a principle of justice but the perpetuation of the law of the strongest and an unwritten code that man has always tried to hide behind "civil" society laws.

For this reason, questioning who could be a rightsholder should scare us because the next step will be the harassment of anyone who is not considered to belong to this group.

The inversion of the perspective of Eusebism is that no man is considered a judge of others of any kind or species.

From my perspective, if anything, we could ask who is "not" a subject of law: in the Eusebist theory, nothing of what exists can be considered a priori devoid of rights; it will be necessary, from time to time, to determine what these rights are and what behaviors are compatible with them.

Once again, everything that exists also includes minerals and plants and animals: in nature, some laws and systems govern everything, regardless of our ability to perceive it.

In general, everything in nature participates in equilibrium, and what is not undergoes penalties that can go as far as its material elimination: this is true for atoms and galaxies and, inevitably, for everything in between these extremes.

Can human rights perhaps require the electron not to orbit around the nucleus of the atom? The rules produced by each system are necessarily directed internally: outside of it, they cannot find justification since any presupposition of them is lacking, above all, sharing, reciprocity, and even knowability.

Individual and Collective Rights

Even the dichotomy of individual rights/collective rights, which fascinates philosophers and jurists so much, must be resolved by reuniting opposites. Expectations, outside of codification, can concern both a single individual and a group.

There has been much debate about whether a right in a technical sense can be attributed to subjects other than the individual, and the most restrictive doctrines recognize the ownership of rights only by human beings in full possession of their mental faculties.

Also, in this case, the distinction between law definition in a technical and nontechnical sense cannot be ignored: rightsholders in the first case are exclusively those identified by the law, while in the second case, the number can be more extensive.

The current law has transposed the concept of widespread rights or collective rights at various levels: in the United States, this is the principle underlying the class action.

The most controversial aspect of collective rights is probably their concrete actuation in court: how can it involve "all" those who have purchased a certain product in a given period? How can you reimburse or compensate all the thousands (or millions!) of consumers if a commodity turns out faulty?

The assumption of collective action is fiction: to pretend that all the individuals of a certain category participate in a judicial action promoted by a few of them.

Here lies the intrinsic limit of collective rights: who can enforce them? Is it necessary for the whole community to act in unison? Is it enough for only a few to act, and if so, which of them? Or should specific representatives of these claims be identified?

We will not go further into the question here since there are many possible solutions, as the variety of legal systems has shown: in any case, these are procedural legislative choices that are not of interest here.

However, what interests us is to frame the relationship between the individual and collective rights at a conceptual level, leaving aside the solutions adopted by the current law.

I believe that we need to recognize collective rights. The term "recognize" means that nothing is invented because it already exists as a fact. Moreover, some interests do not concern only one individual, but entire categories, whose injury determines widespread effects and is sometimes impossible to circumscribe within a given number of subjects.

Releasing a toxic substance into the air does not harm only a single person, nor would it even be possible to identify the directly damaged person; however, this does not mean that the damage has not occurred, but it is much more extensive damage to collective interests.

The criminal sanction imposed in environmental crimes is designed to counteract the injurious action and not compensate for the damage to the bearers of the injured interests.

In such cases, a criminal conviction should also include the obligation to pay compensation, if not in monetary form, through actions aimed at restoring or promoting the rights violated. Thus, for example, those who have polluted should remedy by helping the environment and removing pollution at some level.

In these collective interests, it is also necessary to include nonhuman ones: damage to the environment, for example, has direct consequences toward nature, affecting human and nonhuman animals.

The lack of compensatory actions in the event of damage to collective interests represents a paradox and an undue benefit for the offender: damaging an individual would determine an obligation to compensate, while entire damaging communities would not.

In the industrialized, technological, and globalized world, it has perhaps become easier and more frequent to damage collective interests, rather than individual ones: just think of the introduction of pollutants into the air using vehicles or heating, without counting production or purchase of products made by highly polluting industrial plants.

A right that hides behind the finger of the subjective and personal ownership of rights is contradictory and unjust since it ends up sanctioning conducts that have infinitesimal consequences in an exceptionally more profound way than others, the effects of which have a global reach.

How is it possible to justify the existence of collective rights in the framework of the social contract? Certainly, we cannot speak of a "widespread" manifestation of will in signing a contract, but this limit also applies to all the marginal cases already examined previously, such as infants, the disabled, and such.

In my opinion, the main issue with which the legislative system must deal in the context of collective rights consists of their actuation and, therefore, in identifying the persons entitled to stand in court to obtain compensation.

The most appropriate solution, both from an abstract point of view and in regard to the concrete feasibility, consists of the imposition of penal sanctions based on the principle of restitution. Providing for financial compensation in favor of an association or a community in the case of injuries involving nonhuman animals or the environment does not imply any effective recovery of the damage caused.

Interest-bearing communities are not, nor can they be considered, only human ones: in the case of forest clearing, for example, an environmental association could be compensated, but this would in no way benefit that specific group of trees, nor the nonhuman animals who inhabit it; the only possible relief, in this case, would consist in planting new trees, thus protecting everyone's interests, but being understood that this is not possible concerning the plants that have now been cut down.

In regard to the distinction between rights in a technical and nontechnical sense, we should note that, in the first case, nothing forbids to recognize collective rights; in the second case, considering "rights" as "interests," those that concern an indistinct multitude are the most relevant.

From Anthropocentrism to Econocentrism

Rights are still anthropocentric, and in most (especially Western) countries, the anthropocentrism of law no longer exists: just like humanism, it has been outmoded by econocentrism.

If it is true that the economy is a human construct, just as the underlying interests are human (e.g., making money), it is also true that in this scheme that has been invented, the human being has ended up being overwhelmed, becoming a pawn expendable in the name of the economic interests of others.

We live in a world dominated by the idea that politics, laws, and actions must be based on respect for human beings because of their intellectual or divine primacy (anthropocentrism/humanism). Unfortunately, notwithstanding constitutional papers, nowadays, human beings are subservient to the economy.

Some examples will show the above-said paradigm:

1) Working causes stress, fatigue, limits social relations, implies competition, and is considered by most to be a "necessary" evil. Necessary for what? To make money.
2) Smoking kills. It is a well-known and proven fact, but selling cigarettes is allowed, and manufacturers and governments get money.
3) Pollution kills. The construction and sale of (highly pollutant) smartphones are encouraged by political systems as sources of profit for industry.
4) Many products sold as food cause numerous diseases, but their sale is not prohibited.
5) The clearing of forests to produce paper, furniture, pastures, etc., harms the health of all humanity, but it is not forbidden.

In any case, economic profit prevails over human well-being and even the survival of individuals, entire populations, and even of the same humankind.

From collective to individual choices, little or nothing changes: we choose to give up the company of loved ones to work and thus earn more, we aspire to be richer than others, we let ourselves be bribed, we are inclined to offer our favor to those who are richer in general and can make us rich instead of those who do not offer us any economic income.

Pecunia mensura: the new magnifying glass, everything must be related to the economic dimension in the present. We profess moral values that place our neighbor at the center of everything, yet most of our resources aim to accumulate money rather than pay attention to our fellow men (or those not like us).

Our very morality is imbued with econocentrism since it is in profit that we recognize the supreme good and the goal of every action. Not in man. Not in animals. Not in the environment. In profit.

While money and economy were meant to be simple means, now they are the end and the main goal of our lives. Once they served us, now we serve them.

The economy represents the institutionalization of money. Economic crisis turns into a crisis of values, and the destabilization is not linked to the compromise of a simple means but of the whole system of values.

The case of the Californian drought of recent years is an example of how politics and legislative policy are subordinated not to the well-being of the citizens and communities that they are supposed to represent but to economic interests. Thus, from 2011 to 2015, California has constantly seen its water reserves fall; restrictive measures have been adopted regarding water use by all citizens, but not by economic/productive activities. However, it is precisely these activities that use about 80 percent of the available resources. It is not surprising, then, to ascertain that as much as 50 percent of the water used in California is destined for the breeding of animals for the production of meat, milk, and eggs: nonetheless, the population was instructed to take fewer showers, not to water their gardens, and supplies are rationed, while no action is taken in any way toward the livestock sector, which, moreover, is giving up reserves drawn from groundwater aquifers formed 20,000 years ago.

Even facing economic crisis and drought, both caused by consumerism and industrialization, as well as by animal exploitation, politics and law do not even consider the possibility of changing the model of evolution to which they refer or to question the "value" of money and its role within a society: rather, they sacrifice the direct interests of people to maintain a self-destructive system.

In conclusion, the time of cultural, political, and legal anthropocentrism has passed: this is the era of econocentrism. We should investigate how this happened to revert such a state of things and figure out the next change toward a virtuous and respectful life model.

3.3 LIMITS

A Multispecies Community

Unlike other animal species, humans have designed communities that include more than just members of their own species, feeling at some level the need to share their existence and often also their spaces with many other animals.

Any form of interaction that is not limited to observation represents interference and, as such, an undue and not morally oriented act unless justified by specific reasons.

The so-called domestication consists in the distortion of other species so that they adapt to coexistence with humans: in this, there is nothing altruistic, much less respectful of others' freedom or self-determination, but these are arbitrary acts based on the equation "can = right."

The idea of treating a being "well" (and we know how subjective this concept is) does not necessarily mean respecting it, and if in principle its freedom is not respected, the door is opened to any will. An ideal society does not justify arbitrary acts against anyone or anything.

We do not live in an ideal society. In the real world, in addition to having stolen the habitat of countless species with roads, cities, concrete, logging, and cultivation, we have also decided to introduce individuals of other species into our cities and homes, toward which we are consequently liable.

The same consideration applies to plants and minerals, with which we would, in any case, be led to interact by nature and regardless of the choices of individual communities in given historical periods.

In the contemporary world, understanding who is subject to the law and what rights to protect, even outside the human species, is important because it has incorporated others within its communities.

In an "ideal" world, human laws could take into account only human beings. However, this is not possible in the real world, and these rights must be distributed among all beings subject to human power.

Excluding that "having the possibility to" can be equivalent to "having the right to," is it necessary to ask ourselves what the rights of nonhumans are? In part, this is a false problem since—unlike what humans do—nonhumans have never claimed anything from humans. They have never asked us to do or not to do anything. They have not asked us to transport them on our backs, to fight their wars, to feed them with our meat or to entertain them, etc.

In this sense, it seems that there is a basic misunderstanding when we talk about "animal rights": there is nothing like a dog that claims the right to get food from human beings.

Obligations of this type, which even the welfarist legislation have recognized, can arise only when a human has assumed a responsibility such as the custody of an animal, which at that point depends exclusively on him: this happens because the nonhuman has been deprived of habitat and freedom of choice and, to the extent that a human has imposed his will on him, even simply by deciding to place him in his own home, it is inevitable that he will respond.

The real issue of nonhuman animals is the arbitrary expansion of human rights that necessarily compresses their rights.

I do not dream of a world where human laws deal with nonhuman animals, but a world where there is no need for them and where the animals can simply live by their own rules.

Schizophrenic behaviors that dominate human societies are now evident, and the paradox of "animal rights" is no exception: no species has ever claimed rights against us, while we have arbitrarily stolen resources and spaces from all other species, in addition to deciding who, where, and in what quantity they may exist and, finally, we have included several different species in our communities. At this point, we felt the need to limit what we are allowed toward them, and, immediately, in chorus, numerous voices were raised shouting to the scandal, considering it inadmissible to recognize rights to different species.

I argue that if we are not open to recognizing animal rights, we could limit to discuss human beings' rights in their extension: the global issue about animals is not their claim toward humans, but the limitless exploitation that they suffer.

In general, everybody extends their rights as far as possible, to the point where conflicting stakeholders are not strong enough to protect themselves.

Believing that rights should not be limited when the consequences of actions fall on the environment or nonhuman animals means perpetuating the mind that allowed to make laws that, in the past, allowed men to kill their women, children, or slaves, and such.

Many have argued that human beings cannot take into account nonhumans in their morals and that, therefore, they cannot face any juridical duty as well.

Once again, we should note that it is not about the duties of men, but about limitations to their rights: the most elementary notion of an extension of a right is that it ends where that of others arises.

The question is who is included in the definition of "others": if man creates the (human) law and, therefore, cannot take into consideration what is "other" from these, then any nonhuman entity is outside the scope of human law.

The concept of extraneousness to the universe of law cannot be partial or one-sided: that is, one cannot make claims on one side only, for example, by claiming to extend human rights also to nonhuman animals and the environment, without recognizing to them any right against us.

There is another contradiction: humans would have rights toward beings who cannot fulfill corresponding duties; therefore, we cannot discuss about rights in a technical meaning.

Alien Rights

We have always been accustomed to considering human laws as the supreme and absolute source of law, facilitated in this above all because all other terrestrials are speechless, technologically less advanced, and, consequently, unable to oppose human decisions.

How would our law deal with different species that aren't "inferior" (as the animals) but "superior"?[13] Could we extend our precepts to them or demand them to obey?

Let us imagine that a sentient alien species, technologically more advanced than us, comes to Earth, claiming the right to possess the planet based on the following assumptions:

i) Intellectual and evolutionary primacy.
ii) Technological primacy.
iii) Military primacy.

If the rights (in the nontechnical sense) were a mere prerogative of a human society, there would be no argument to oppose the alien species to persuade it peacefully to renounce the dominion of the Earth; all rights, starting from the fundamentals, as created (and not only implemented) by human beings, would be unenforceable and inapplicable to an alien species.

Contractualism would not help, considering that alien species never entered into any agreement with humans.

Going deeper in the matter, we can argue that the reasons for aliens' rights reflect those adduced by humanity to found their right to dispose of everything that exists.

In the movie *Wang's Arrival*,[14] we can see an interspecies confrontation between humans and extraterrestrials. When humans torture the alien creature, one dissents, arguing that they are not respecting his human rights: the commander immediately replies that the creature, being nonhuman, is not eligible for human rights.

If anything showed in the movie ever happens, we could figure two possibilities: warlike aliens would be able to impose their claims by force, while peaceful extraterrestrials more evolved than humans would be forced to fight for their rights, just as all human minorities did in the past.

If there were no "right" way of acting or any rights other than what the laws sanctioned by the society affirm, there would be no legal basis to support, even among human beings themselves, the principle of equality and non-discrimination. The human right would undoubtedly find an insurmountable limit to its applicability toward more advanced extraterrestrial species, based on legal positivism; on the other hand, recognizing the fundamental right of self-determination as innate and inviolable, the solution would be easy. By simply resorting to a universal principle such as respect for free will, even a situation unforeseen by any legislator would be easily resolved, ensuring peaceful coexistence between species at different evolutionary levels, rather than enslaving some to others.

Limits to Acting Toward Yourself

There are many different approaches of the law toward individual's self-disposal acts. Endless debates persist in determining what is lawful and what is not and, therefore, what laws should allow or prohibit.

This is one of the most heterogeneous and variable issues in the law, depending on the geographical areas and cultural contexts.

Typically, controversial issues are the right to abortion, suicide, euthanasia, and medical treatment. In many of these cases, there is the contradiction and hypocrisy of a society which, for example, considers not only correct, but sometimes even a moral duty to "sterilize" pets or give them a "sweet death" in case of illness, but who strongly repudiate such acts toward other humans.

From an ethical point of view, I cannot find any justification for abortion, considering that science has now ascertained the development and awareness of the fetus in periods even earlier than the threshold allowed by the law, which varies from country to country.

Respecting the right to life also implies respecting legitimate expectations and taking into account suffering.

It would be reductive to address the issue of abortion only from the unborn child's perspective.

First of all, it is also necessary to take into consideration the free will of the parents and, in particular, of the mother, who is the one who would face the pregnancy materially: if, on the one hand, the prohibition to interrupt it privileges the right to life of the unborn child, on the other hand, it establishes a sort of obligation to do, that is, to face the entire gestation and childbirth itself.

There is, then, a further aspect: the unborn child has not only the right to life, but also the right not to suffer, and to forbid a woman to practice abortion is equivalent to taking responsibility for the existence to come but for which it is not the legislator or the "critics" to take charge.

The right to live at all costs can legitimately be contrasted with the right to live peacefully, happily, and without abstract preclusions to pursue individual evolution.

After inhibiting the potential mother from abortion, the problem is: will she be responsible for guaranteeing all the above to the unborn child?

In my opinion, the government cannot interfere in such issues, considering the repercussions on people's lives.

Before addressing the apparent ethical dilemma of human abortion, the law should disregard any form of violence and killing of everything that is not human, and the so-called forms of "population control," which consist of real massacres against nonhuman species deemed overpopulated or overcrowded concerning available resources.

Life, which is usually considered the highest good, is characterized not only by length but—above all—by quality. Saying that it is immoral to allow suicide to someone suffering and dying has nothing to do with the philosophically understood morality but with religious assumptions of various kinds.

From a philosophical perspective, it is unacceptable to force someone to endure suffering, leading to death rather than interrupting life.

I do not think that stopping suffering represents a correct choice; however, I believe that the decision in this regard must be entirely left to each person's free will.

The flattening of existence to the mere biological phenomenon called "life" is contradictory even based on religious beliefs: anyone who believes in a spiritual existence cannot justify the attachment to simple biological life "whatever it takes."

Even atheists and those who do not believe in the soul's survival cannot rationally justify the artificial continuation of life when it is devoid of awareness or characterized by extreme suffering.

Whether a person believes or not, in any case, it is not clear why the law can discipline such an intimate and profound question.

Also, in this case, there is an incredible dichotomy between the behavior toward other species and ours; in fact, how would it be possible to say that it is good to "kill" a sick animal while condemning a human to suffer? This is yet another example of schizophrenia, that is, making different decisions despite the identity of the assumptions.

In general, the legal obligations relating to individual conduct whose effects only concern the agent are attributable to moral principles. However, morality is not something universally shared, and even if there were universal precepts, not everyone shares them.

I can see no justification in the imposition of moral conduct through laws, except in the case of conduct whose effects affect subjects other than the agent.

Limitations of rights to acting toward oneself should be rejected in principle. The issue is not whether the society or the legislator shares the individual's choices, but they must allow them.

Although entirely carried out by individuals, there is a category of behaviors considered to fall on the entire community: there are numerous restrictions on personal freedom since the collective interest is placed before it.

Often the interest of the community is not material or contingent, but moral: just think of the laws on morality, which are strongly affected by culture, especially religion.

Just figure the paradox of dressing: no animal in the world was born "dressed," and no animal in the world feels modesty in being naked. Only humans are able to experience such feelings.

Is this perhaps an intrinsic and innate characteristic of our species? If this were the case, it would not explain why ancient cultures or nontechnological societies of our times did not feel modesty in nudity: just think of the Greek Olympics, in which athletes competed completely naked without causing any confusion in the crowd that attended the competitions.

How is it possible that something considered shocking today was normal 2,500 years ago? What has changed in us since then? Many things, but one in particular: religion.

Thinking of the Christian religion's obscurantism that led to mutilating ancient statues to cover up their "shame" makes us smile today, or rather, it would do so if we did not still live with the consequences of that mentality.

We frequently see images of naked people censored; meanwhile, showing guns or wars is allowed.

Limiting the expression of nature (naked bodies) while allowing the celebration of death and killing lies on a hypocritical moral.

Actions involving or favoring the spread of diseases, economic hardships, or real material damage can be legitimately limited by a law, while the mere fact of feeling uncomfortable with others' self-expressions cannot justify any law remedy.

Limits to Acting Toward Others

The basic statement about rights is "one's rights end where others' begin." From a philosophical perspective, it is fundamental to ascertain who the "others" are.

If we used the technical-legal terminology, the existence of a right could be extremely easy to ascertain: like the two possible positions of an on/off switch, so it would exist if and only as recognized by the laws.

If we were to refer to the law in the nontechnical sense, speaking, for example, of expectations, things would get complicated: how is it possible to know the expectations of others? The current law bypasses the question, taking into account only the legally acknowledged claims and, thus, homologating and standardizing any individual expectation. Among citizens subject to the same laws, should we conclude that the actions of one respect the right of the others when complying with laws?

The extension of rights is more complicated when people subject to different legal systems interact: in this case, it is fundamental to establish who the "other" is, and whose expectations can mark the boundary of the extension of ours.

The simplest—but also the most superficial—solution is to deny relevance to all those who do not participate in the social contract. Here comes the paradox, according to which everything that is not human is considered the object of human rights, but in turn, not eligible as rightsholder.

This solution is unjustified whether it is legal in a technical or nontechnical sense: in the first case, there can be no adhesion, no reciprocity, and no assumption of duties, while in the second case, everyone's expectations should be taken into consideration, not only those of the strongest.

Recognizing the expectations of others presupposes that they are intelligible to the observer, but this is possible only at certain basic levels: for example, one can imagine that any animal has an interest in continuing its existence and not suffering, but one cannot expect to know if a specific individual in any given moment feeds the expectation of eating, or drinking or sleeping, and such.

We can conclude that our expectations can be legitimately pursued and eventually satisfied if this does not damage the expectations of others and vice versa. But which "others" are relevant in this evaluation? To avoid discrimination and prejudice, the only possible answer is everything other than us.[15]

How to translate the principles of a pure law into a current law? Simply by limiting what each can have within the boundaries of its citizens and excluding any unnecessary/avoidable interference from the scope of rights.

In legal terms, the well-known principle according to which "everything that is not expressly prohibited is permitted" can only be applied within the rights available, that is, people's rights stated by the law.

Regarding nonhuman animals and the environment, the only conducts admissible by the law should be those inspired by necessity and nonavoidability, without prejudice to compliance with the principle of equilibrium: exploitation for economic purposes, the violence of any kind, hunting, fishing, eating meat are not justifiable.

How could the law justify using pesticides, rat poisons, insecticides, and such? Do those creatures have to die because they somehow violated human laws? Perhaps they would have entered some sort of social contract with humankind? Perhaps the human desire to get nice fruits or cities and countryside without mice or annoying insects should prevail over the expectation of those creatures to survive?

And what about the breeding of animals for food purposes or experimentation? It is not about recognizing rights to nonhuman subjects but simply recognizing the actual limits of human rights. These limits depend on the fact that our species makes our rules, so they cannot cross it. We should respect the statement, "Anything that is not expressly forbidden by society is permitted to its members."

In the Middle Ages, nonhumans were prosecuted: this, which apparently might seem absurd, instead demonstrates greater consistency concerning today's law, which would never allow prosecuting nonhumans, while they can be (and actually are) condemned, without due process.

There are dogs condemned to death for biting children or human adults, while many strays are exterminated worldwide. We also systematically kill insects with atrocious methods (the common insecticide paralyzes them, leaving them to die of starvation).

The first known trial case against nonhumans dates to 864 AD, when the Diet of Worms sentenced a swarm of bees, guilty of killing a man, to death by smoking[16]: compared to then, the only difference is that today the sentence would come without any trial.

We almost smile, thinking of pigs, dogs, or even earthworms in the dock. However, we should instead be horrified at a present that, considering it unthinkable to subject nonhuman individuals to trial, instead considers it natural to apply measures of any kind to them, including administration of death, in a completely arbitrary way.

If we agree that the "other," to be included in our moral and legal obligations, is everything else from ourselves, we can define limitations to our rights based on reciprocity. Even in this case, the current law seems schizophrenic: just think about two human behaviors like listening to music and driving a car, both of which are permitted. Listening to music is lawful if it does not interfere with the neighbor's right to silence: when the trespass occurs, the generically admitted conduct becomes prohibited, and the law imposes a sanction. The interests in question are of the same level: on the one hand, the pleasure of music and, on the other hand, that of silence or quiet.

Let us now consider the example of driving a car: on the one hand, the interest of the individual in moving and, on the other hand, the interest of other humans in health. Around 200 years ago, cars didn't exist, yet the human species had already prospered on Earth for millennia: I would hardly say that driving is a fundamental interest or a necessary activity. But, on the other hand, health and survival are undoubtedly superordinate interests: how then to justify this disparity of treatment by the law conceptually? If I annoy a neighbor with loud music, I can be fined or even arrested (in some countries), while if I make pollution or endanger pedestrians by driving, causing disease and (potential) death, I commit a lawful act and am not subject to any sanctions.

There is, then, a basic problem of the law: the prevalence of economic rights over fundamental rights, as understood in accordance with laws and constitutions.

Although on paper it is generally expected that economic interests are subordinate to those considered fundamental such as, first and foremost, life and health, in practice, the legal systems do not respect these precepts in the least; rather, they subvert them.

In the globalized world of multinationals, it is permissible to consume thousands of liters of water just to make a t-shirt or a hamburger or cut down forests only to create pastures for livestock. This is made to get rich by selling mostly superfluous things after convincing others of their usefulness.

How could a system that allows an entrepreneur to steal energy and collective resources be reconciled with the law and with fundamental rights, producing pollution and products aimed at his exclusive profit, with damage to public health? It is simple: it cannot be reconciled in any way.

If the laws allow all this, the fundamental principles of law and the proclamation that the rights of one end where the rights of the others arise are sterile words on wastepaper, contradicted by a reality established and endorsed by those same rules which, for internal consistency, should have been prevented.

Many "advanced" countries, affirming human rights, made it easier and cheaper for companies to produce in other countries, where people are almost enslaved to guarantee low-cost labor. The same happens with electric vehicles or electronic devices, usually considered ecological, while they heavily impact parts of the world where most consumers cannot see.

Also, in this case, the current national law cannot be enforced, since exploitation takes place outside national borders; however, allowing the exercise of economic activities, even if only for resale and distribution, of goods made abroad without respecting fundamental rights, means to legitimize against others all those conducts that are prohibited toward one's associates.

There is and cannot be any consistency in a one-way system, tolerating or endorsing harmful behavior to the detriment of others and condemning or repressing and punishing those to their detriment.

3.4 WHAT RIGHTS?

There is much talk about human and animal rights, less about environmental ones, but in doing so, one of the most common limits is that many of these rights are never examined in detail.

The question is fundamental since establishing in practice the rights of each person is necessary to affirm them: how can something unknown or uncertain be instituted? Those who approach the subject for the first time might think that the solution is understood and that refusing discrimination means treating everyone differently, but this would be impossible: how can one behave equally between a human being and stone?

Rejecting discrimination means treating similar situations in the same way and not treating different situations in the same way, representing a kind of reverse discrimination.

Questioning about a cat's right to vote or about a tree's right to property would be unreasonable, but this does not mean that they cannot enjoy rights in a nontechnical sense, corresponding, in a technical sense, to limitations of human rights.

Before examining the content of rights according to each category, it is worth asking whether it is necessary to refer to the concept of rights or not.

The Need of the Right

Not everyone agrees on the need for the right as a tool for affirmation of claims: for example, the ecofeminist movement opposes them with the ethics of relationships, that is, a system of values that rejects the absolutes and requires that each case be treated as a separate case, determining from time to time the appropriate conduct to guarantee respect for the other subject.

The rule of conduct could never be disconnected from single individuals; therefore, it could not refer to either a species or a genus in its entirety: this would exclude discrimination a priori and would also make it unnecessary to resort to general codified rights, which do not hold any (or, at least, in due) consideration of specificities.

These are antithetical perspectives concerning the history of human civilization, which from its origins to today has constantly sought to extend the system of rights, constantly including new institutions, categories, and subjects; of course, the mere fact that this has happened so far does not mean that it is correct or necessary.

At some level, not necessarily the technical one, the law is not a human creation: as highlighted by Bekoff and Pierce, all communities of individuals need and aspire by nature to order that guarantees its continuity.[17]

We use to link the idea of legitimate expectation, injury, and corresponding punishment to what we call "right in the technical sense": we can change the name, but the substance would be the same.

We can also discuss how to recognize and whether to codify this set of claims and punishments, but—as we said before—even lions and wolves apply a form of justice based on legitimate expectations and punishments.

Considering that the rules and sanctions are innate in us, as in all animals, it is much more important to determine their content or application methods rather than discussing the most appropriate name for them.

On the other hand, not even those who, like the feminist echoes, dispute the law deny that everyone has legitimate expectations to be protected, but this is the right!

In the above, he helps Bobbio, who has correctly identified the distinction between the rights that have already been recognized by the legal system and those that, on the other hand, are still simple claims, distinguishing them into strong and weak rights.[18]

It is difficult to bring a civil or administrative law back to similar "natural" analogies. In this case, we deal with artificial conventions so closely linked to the historical and sociocultural context that they differ in each nation, even significantly.

In this regard, it is also correct to observe differences between human and nonhuman animals and that our specificities have made such a massive set of rules. This is an issue because the perfect state does not have many laws: it does not need laws at all. The more laws a country needs, the less advanced it is.

Human Rights

Legal relativism is the doctrine that, excluding natural law, attributes exclusive importance to the associates' will, and, therefore, to the sociocultural and historical context in making rights and laws.

I partially agree with this statement because it is impossible to find the roots to the whole legal system in nature, especially in an increasingly complex society like ours: in this context, the only wish may be to simplify relations and thus make most of the rules superfluous. Today, it is a simple utopia, but I do not doubt that humanity's distant future holds this.

Since the human being has more complex relationships than any other terrestrial, the number and type of rights are also maximum, and, inevitably, most of them cannot find any analogy outside the human species.

Regarding fundamental rights, I believe that recognizing their origin in the legislative system is an inadmissible vicious circle: we affirm that they are inalienable, but how could this be if they were justified only in the will that a community has expressed in a given historical moment? If this were the case, even the right to life could simply be abrogated following the change in mentality.

In the strict sense of the word, the basic fundamental rights are only freedom and self-determination: all the others, although called "rights," represent limits to the actions of others.

Considering the state as a subject, which must comply with certain obligations toward its associates, is artificial. But, outside of these artificial subjects, even those who make up the constitutions consider fundamental rights to be nothing more than negative rights that do not allow for any positive action to be required but only limits to the actions of others.

As enforced in many countries worldwide, the fundamental right to health allows any citizen to claim care from the government (e.g., drugs, hospitals, cures). At the same time, and based on the same right to health, each of us can expect that other individuals do not harm their health through harmful behaviors. Therefore, we can conclude that it is contradictory to support the affirmation of positive rights, legitimizing the demand for the fulfillment of others, while not even basic negative rights are recognized and enforced.

If we consider all rights as a mere invention made by rulers, then—for example—if a country allows slavery, other countries cannot make any objection: what problem would there be in importing goods manufactured by slaves into a nation that do you consider lawful?

How could we say that a country is violating "human rights" if it had not recognized them at all?

We somehow "feel" that something is wrong in the above, but legal positivism cannot support us in our claim because even the so-called fundamental rights can be determined only by the rulers: if they decide that life is not a right, then it is not.

The very recent history of humanity provides the most extreme conclusion of absolute relativism: how could we say that racial laws were unjust? If we adopt the norm itself as a just or unjust parameter, this is simply impossible. Anything that the law prescribes would be right.

This is what happens if we fail to identify innate principles such as natural laws.

Legal positivism, denying natural laws, fails to consider that not all rights are fundamental and that most current laws are the mere specification of broader genres.

We can foresee that, in the future, there will be rights different from ours, just as ours differ from the past; this does not mean that we cannot recognize the fundamental nucleus of rights or expectations innate in each human being. Different sociocultural and historical contexts impose different definitions based on rulers' needs and people's feelings.

The innate, or natural, right can be considered a mannequin, while all the other rights represent clothes with which this can be dressed: they can have any fabric, shape, and color, but no one could stand without the mannequin.

I suggest that every legal system is built on the principles of respect and equilibrium: at an international level, this could be described as reciprocity.

The principle of equality results from freedom and self-determination, as classifying, by legislative means, categories of superior or privileged individuals concerning others would represent an undue interference with those placed arbitrarily at the lower levels.

Nor can we consider applying these concepts within national boundaries since this would mean disapplying them outside of them, failing to recognize their universality.

Respect, freedom, and self-determination also lead to considering necessary some rights that our laws have not yet taken into consideration and that, in the future, will appear more and more fundamental: if one occupies a land, beyond housing "needs," it automatically compresses everyone else's ability to do the same; if someone, to get rich, cuts down a forest to establish a pasture, all the others have less air to breathe; if some pollute the atmosphere or the seas, all the others are harmed.

Contemporary lawmakers argue about respect for the human person and his highest values but neglect what is essential: in the United States, the right to carry a firearm is considered a fundamental expression of the freedom of individuals, while it goes completely unnoticed that thousands of industries poison the air, water, and earth.

What is the use of setting limits on the pollution permitted by the law if it is known that every form of pollution harms others? For example, what is the use of banning child labor within one's borders when national companies outsource production to other countries of the world that allow child exploitation?

What fundamental and inalienable rights does a nation recognize, whose economy is based on exploiting the resources of weaker, systematically impoverished, and plundered countries, as often happens between Western and emerging countries?

And how can we talk about the right to health, in a health system that subsidizes the drug industry, responsible for more diseases than it promises to cure, in which substances harmful to the body are sold at staggering prices, while manufacturers enrich and people impoverish, only to see their health decline?

About the penal system, respect for the fundamental rights of the person requires that recourse to measures restricting freedom be considered an evil that is necessary only to avoid the danger of recurrence of conduct that damages the equally fundamental rights of other citizens. In contrast, for all other violations, we should provide deterrent sanctions, which in addition to this purpose are also therapeutic and educational.

Many Western countries, including the United States, have penal systems not limited to punishing criminals through deprivation of liberty, but also aimed at restoring community or the damaged individuals what they have been deprived of, in addition to "re-educating" the offenders.

Excluding the moralistic concept of criminal justice "*punietur quia peccatum est*" (punishing because they sinned), the full application of the "*punietur ne peccetur*" (punishing to avoid sinning) principle presupposes both the effectiveness of the sentence and the adoption of re-educational measures aimed at really guaranteeing that the offenders do not repeat their unlawful conduct.

Prisoning has the effect of preventing the convict from repeating offenses, but only for the time of imprisonment. Thus, the community does not benefit from it, while it is forced to bear huge costs for implementing and maintaining the prison systems.

The rehabilitative purpose of imprisonment has always remained a dead letter, because it is also not possible to create such a complex system without providing for any actual principle.

An efficient criminal justice system must start with the prevention and teaching of its principles and rules to all community members to have practical knowledge of it and understand and share its deeper aims.

In compliance with the fundamental principles of law, the deprivation of liberty can only be a residual and extreme solution. In any case, it should be applied together with scrupulously planned rehabilitation techniques and not left to chance or the goodness of the individual prison institution.

Prisoners should first deal with the consequences of their actions, the pain and deprivation caused to their victims, and undertake paths to increase their awareness, the reasons that led them to commit a crime, and the alternative solutions offered to them. Who, for example, has committed crimes due to a state of poverty or the inability to support themselves otherwise?

Conversely, all the rights currently recognized by the legal systems in force, and which encroach on the rights of others, cannot be affirmed, both for all the moral reasons relating to the affirmation of fundamental rights and for political and pragmatic issues: a world cannot be just if the principles on which the order is based are themselves betrayed.

Fundamental rights can all be considered with “innate” expectations, that is, those that each average individual has toward his neighbor, regardless of the conditioning of a positive law.

If we accept pure legal relativism, we should conclude that there is no innate expectation in the human being: this is not. The facts contradict it, but it would be completely illogical considering that even nonhuman animals have similar expectations. It would be contradictory and paradoxical to affirm that the human species is the most evolved and lacks even the basic expectations typical of any mammal.

If, for example, while walking down the street, another person attacked us without reason, we would feel a deep sense of injustice, which would be lessened if, before the attack, we had provoked the other with insults and threats; if we were the first to use violence, we would feel no sense of injustice at all for having suffered it in our turn.

In the first two cases, our “feeling” would be in accordance with the law, while in the third, it would not. Yet, this discrepancy would not attenuate the sense of injustice or justice: these perceptions derive precisely from something that, although variable and subjective, is innate in all of us and allows us to talk about expectations, the violation of which is considered as a lack of respect.

The accessory/artificial rights are characterized by determining a corresponding sense of justice rather than codifying an innate one. Thus, for example, if we were driving by car along a road and someone, running through a red light, crashes into us, we would feel that we are victims of injustice not based on an innate expectation, but only because of the traffic rules in force in that place.

In its exceptional complexity, human coexistence also implies the use of accessory/artificial rights, but this does not mean that the number of fundamental rights, as some argued, is constantly changing or that there are no natural rights either.

A common mistake made by critics of natural law is not realizing that we can consider an infinite amount of rights "fundamental," but this does not mean that they are.

Human rights should tend toward constant improvement, which means that at the end of their evolution, they should fully reflect moral demands and, therefore, law and ethics should coincide.

We can imagine that, in the future, imprisonment is abolished in the name of the right to personal freedom: this would not be a new right but a new derivation from an existing right.

Among the many rights considered fundamental and perhaps even traced back to hypothetical laws of nature, one deserves separate mention for its total equivocality: the property right.

The need for ownership arises from the human tendency to act out of selfishness and seek the fulfillment of unnecessary desires. If a community were to sustain itself entirely by cultivating limited land, the most functional solution would be to distribute the fruits equally to have a quantity like that of the others.

Everything stems from a misunderstanding: that things are immutable as if we (owners) and the object of our claims (property) are fixed and eternal, but this is not the case since everything changes sooner or later.

Property is simply an artifice of law, which cannot change the physics laws: can a law prohibit the land from being submerged by the sea? Or a tornado of not wiping out a city? Or to a person not to die?

There is no such thing as an absolute right to things since they nor we are absolute and, regardless of beliefs about the afterlife, we leave this world the same way we entered it: we introduce nothing, we take nothing away.

How, then, could we be the master of something that preexisted us and that will persist after our disappearance?

We are all simply users of what exists, for the short time that we are allowed: it may change the extent and duration of use, but not the fact that it is limited both for what the laws define as owner and for the owner, holder, etc.

It is also necessary to distinguish between natural things and artificial things: pretending to exercise rights toward nature is another manifestation of anthropocentric culture. We, human beings, are usually unable to recognize scopes different from ours, and we are completely deaf and blind toward expectations and rights outside those who have the voice to shout them and the strength to affirm them.

Nature cannot be possessed for the same reason that people or animals cannot (today) be possessed (unfortunately in the latter case, a positive law has not yet arrived at this finding): everything that exists has the same origin as all the others, even if it manifests itself in different forms.

Any use of assets limits the use of others; therefore, if everyone is limited to satisfying their own needs, everyone can participate equally, while if some use more than is necessary, others are unable to satisfy even the fundamental needs.

For artificial objects, the question arises in different terms since they are created for specific purposes and could hardly be used for others. In this case, we should analyze the production to determine if anyone can grab the natural resources necessary to make such objects, thus taking them away from all other terrestrials.

Animal Rights

Humans are entitled to innate rights given by nature and to artificial rights that they have established, while nonhuman animals are entitled only to natural rights: as we said, our legal system should not, in any way, involve them.

Life, freedom, and self-determination: these are the fundamental rights that belong to nonhumans and from which all the corresponding duties of respect on our part arise.

The right to life includes that to health, as the latter is strictly connected to the same quality and expectation as the first: we cannot harm nor dispose of those who cannot express their will. Usually, we consider the lack of speech as an excuse to do what we want, while the inability to express consent can never be considered equivalent to an assent.

Any practice involving the injury or killing of other animals is illegitimate, and this involves killing "inferior" animal life forms, such as insects. We are used to considering insects expendables during our many activities, and every time they interfere with or harass us.

The only concern regarding the massacre of insects caused by humans is related to the ecosystem: this happens for the disappearance of bees.

The most aberrant manifestation of anthropocentrism toward animals consists of the practice of vivisection, which its supporters undertake to define "experimentation" so that popular culture considers it an outdated practice that is alive and well (i.e., precisely, dissecting live animals).

However, the issues of the definition of experimentation are futile: animals used for the experiments experience many deprivations, harms, and, then, they usually die. This is more than enough to conclude that being alive or not during dissection does not change things.

The whole life of these individuals—and I emphasize "individuals" to specify that they are sentient creatures, each with their sensitivity, character, and exclusive thoughts—takes place inside cages with completely unnatural circadian rhythms and nutrition decided by the breeders first and then by experimenters.

It would be impossible and useless to review the exhaustive list of cruelties perpetrated against laboratory guinea pigs: it is enough to remember that they include: interventions, mutilation, inoculation of bacteria, viruses, induced lesions, insertion of electrodes or prostheses, genetic manipulation, behavioral, dissection, pulping, inhalation of substances of all kinds, poisoning, removal of organs and tissues, fractures, etc.

The only real liberation is death.

Just as none of us would accept to be exploited or sacrificed either for one's fellow man or a more evolved alien species, no reason can ethically justify the deprivation of many other animals' freedom, self-determination, and life itself, just for our benefit, pleasure, or gain.

Usefulness is completely irrelevant: who of us would like to be tortured and killed to help others?

Equally, the fact of knowing that a serial killer is relieved, and therefore his quality of life improves, thanks to killing, would hardly interest us: all we would like to do is not to become his victim, regardless of the benefits he might derive from it. But, on the other hand, suppose vivisection demands attention due to the variety of tortures invented and practiced. In that case, the cornerstone of respect for the life of nonhuman animals is the abstention from their use for food purposes, which is not—as many believe—the result of a choice of extreme love or unusual generosity; indeed, it is not a choice at all, at least no more than it is not to kill other humans.

Even nowadays, most people believe that humans eat other animals by nature and that, in any case, it is a biological necessity: this is far from the truth.

Human beings are essentially frugivorous, but we could (perhaps) morally justify killing animals if we needed to feed on meats. However, there is no way to justify the systematic killing of billions of nonhumans by a few individuals who get money from this.

How to justify the forced fattening of geese until their livers burst to obtain *foie gras*? Or the bile bears, who in China spend all the years of their thankless lives immobilized in cages and force-fed while a catheter extracts the bile they produce?

Or again, still in Japan, eating live frogs?

In ethical terms, there is a substantial difference between carrying out an action dictated by existential necessity and carrying it out for simple ambition, which undoubtedly is enrichment, but also between the consumption of necessary (or presumed) "foods" and others that, even in the awareness of the proponents of omnivorous behavior, have no use, but represent mere charms.

Eating animals is not only superfluous but seriously harmful to humans, and, therefore, the justification of need is yet another reason in favor of veganism or, better, of fruitarianism.

But even if all the above were false and erroneous, there would still be very good reasons to argue that it is wrong to preclude nonhumans from the right to live in the name of our livelihood: considering that the vegan choice is possible, this is already enough to make it morally dutiful, as it causes less suffering to other animals, to humans themselves, and less damage to the environment.

Although less harmful to himself than food, man has invented another use of nonhumans, equally useless and cruel: to exploit skins and furs for clothes, furnishings, and decorations.

The fact that not even the use of animals for such futile purposes is prohibited shows no real legislative implementation of ethical principles. At the same time, anthropocentrism and econocentrism are only confirmed: if it satisfies our society and its purposes of profit, however useless and cruel, everything is lawful.

Unlike the food issue, probably nobody can consider using nonhumans to create clothes or shoes as necessary, while we are all perfectly aware that these are ephemeral satisfactions.

The tannery industry transforms fabrics destined for rapid decay into clothes, accessories, and furnishings through the massive use of highly polluting and toxic synthetic chemicals: the result of these manipulations, harmful to animals, the environment, and (therefore) humans, is promoted as a synonym of quality, durability, and high social standing. In contrast, countless plant or synthetic substances have far superior characteristics.

In recent decades, the world has often mobilized at various levels, including through prominent personalities and associations, against the use of furs, deploring the suffering inflicted on minks, foxes, seals, and such, destined to be raised in cages, or caught with the use of leghold traps, or, worse still, slaughtered with sticks or the like.

The mobilization against the use of furs is certainly acceptable, but in ethical terms, there is no reason why a leather suit is to be justified more than a fur coat: whether there is hair or not, in both cases, we are inflicting deprivation of freedom, suffering, and death.

Distinguishing between analogous phenomena can be the result of ignorance, hypocrisy, or simple naivety, but any in-depth analysis can only lead to the conclusion that a pair of shoes or a leather handbag, from an ethical point of view, is completely equivalent to a fur coat, as well as to a leather sofa or a silk scarf.

Some question the use of wool, considering that it does not imply killing the animal.

Even with the necessary distinctions, wool production is to that of leather as milk production is to that of meat: in both cases, there is exploitation that involves suffering and the constraint of nonhumans that humans don't hesitate in the killing.

Of course, one can argue about how much better the existence of a "wool" sheep, outdoors and for pastures, is compared to that of a "dairy" cow, locked up and forced to procreate and produce milk until exhaustion, but these are quantitative, not qualitative, differences.

If the duty is not to cause suffering, it cannot be justified by affirming that one conduct causes little suffering or less than another: the latter may certainly be more deplorable, but the former cannot be right.

With a little effort of empathy, we can better understand the meaning of our "mitigating circumstances" when presented with the hypothesis of justifying one behavior that we recognize as harmful. For example, if someone imprisoned us and injured us slightly, we would certainly be happier than if imprisoned and tortured heavily, but could we say that we are happy?

Our duty is not to realize the happiness of others, which is something supererogatory, but it is certainly not to cause them unhappiness. In addition to life and health, the rights to freedom and self-determination are fundamental.

The question of animal rights must be separated between domestic and wild ones: respect for the fundamental rights of the former implies ceasing their use, while for the latter, we must include respect toward the environment.

The fundamental prerequisite for exercising these rights is habitat: without an environment that offers the space and resources to live, reproduce, move, feed, and shelter, what freedom can nonhuman animals have? How can they self-determine in a world dominated by the human species, which decides which places to relegate them, and how many to take, kill, sterilize, or exploit in various ways?

Because of animal farming, thousands of species are deprived of the forest, and therefore of their life, produce food for cattle, while thousands and millions of other animals suffer and die as a direct consequence. Simply to collect palm oil, entire forests are razed to the ground to cultivate this plant that provides yet another useless gastronomic tinsel of Western countries.

The rampant overbuilding has mutilated and continues to mutilate the planet at an unstoppable pace, not only depriving other species of their habitat, but even replacing it with infinite dangers, pollution, and devastation: within these places we call cities, then, not satisfied with the above, we capture, and we imprison other animals in circuses, zoos, aquariums, kennels, catteries, etc.

Western societies consider the house a fundamental right of the person, but they do not care if, building second, third, and fourth houses, all the other species, even those who need just a tree to call home, are on the way for extinction.

How can we talk about animal rights without affirming the duty to limit the human impact on the environment? Direct killing apart, we do not even allow animals to come into existence, destroying their habitats.

As for freedom and self-determination, I believe that domestication also represents an undue interference in the existence of other species: interactions between individuals, regardless of the species they belong to, should only take place on a mutually voluntary basis and not because the strongest determines where and as the weakest should live.

The best example of human selfishness is the so-called best friend: none of today's dog breeds were born in nature, but they result from genetic selections of the last centuries.[19]

The gifts we made to our companion include distortion and sick breeds affected by innate pathologies such as respiratory disorders, walking defects, deformities, disproportions, etc.

We put our pets in concrete, iron, marble, and glass structures, and we distort their diet, feeding them on other animals!

What ethical basis is there in preferring one animal's life to another just because it is closer to us? Of course, none of us are obliged to live with other animals of any species, but the fact that we decide to do so does not automatically entitle us to use other animals: the fact that my child needs a liver transplant does not make it lawful for me to take one from my neighbor. There is no reason, save for our selfishness, that leads us to favor the interests of those we have at heart, which allows us to affirm the duty to support someone while at the same time giving ourselves the right to kill others for this purpose.

Also, to avoid the serious moral conflicts caused by our actions, it is essential to affirm as a priority the duty to limit our consumption (mostly waste) of resources and territory, returning them to all other terrestrials.

We should consider the present a transitory situation, destined to change when the actions correspond to ethics: it is impossible to act in the absolute best possible way in the transitional period, but the lesser evil principle must inspire us.

It is not important whether the highest good is achievable today, but it is essential to become aware of the ultimate objectives: naturally, they cannot coincide with the present customs, since in this case, we would live in a perfect society that does not require any transformation.

In this transitional period, it is necessary to strive to achieve the greatest possible respect for the rights of animals, first by limiting all forms of disposition toward them, starting from the removal of habitats.

By abolishing trade and equating them with property or objects, the legal conditions for their systematic killing for food or any other purpose would also disappear. Moreover, any experimentation based on breeding, sale, deprivation of liberty, injury, and killing would also be impossible on the same premises.

At the end of this very long and painful journey, the human being will be able to declare the end of the war, devious and fratricidal, which for millennia of its existence has opposed it to all its nonhuman peers.

Environmental Rights

Usually, the question is how it is possible to attribute rights to the environment. Before answering a question, we should always ask ourselves if it has been formulated correctly: in this case, I do not think so. I think the right question to ask is: "How would it be possible to attribute rights to human beings without doing the same with the environment?"[20]

The atoms and molecules that make up each of us come from and are destined to return to the universe and the Earth that provided them to us and of which they are made up: that matter is constantly changing, but it never disappears.

Today we discuss the rights of the fetus and the unborn child, but how could that future person ever develop and come into existence without the possibility for the mother to breathe the matter in the form of gas present in the atmosphere or without being able to ingest solids and liquids, which in turn were formed and developed from the combination of other atoms and molecules?

All of us are made up, in varying parts, of minerals and metals spread on Earth, of the carbon that infinitesimal bacteria have produced, or of the oxygen synthesized by plants that existed billions of years before us.

If someone had denied the right to exist in that primordial soup hypothesized by Oparin, what would be of us all today?

How can we say that a set of molecules has rights, but the larger set of molecules from which it derives has none?

It would be a contradiction to deny rights to the environment without denying them to ourselves.

As I said, we have chosen (arbitrarily) parameters to determine what is alive and what is not: based on that arbitrary decision, we then made classifications to establish what is eligible for rights and what is not.

Quite coincidentally, the human being is, according to the majority (of humans), the only rightsholder, or, at least, of the "real" ones, that is, those that allow him to demand respect and obtain something else as compensation when this is not the case. But, unfortunately, we continue to feed these misunderstandings, building houses of cards on false premises.

We cannot refuse the (alleged) will of nature and pretend to replace it with laws based on the will of man: we, in flesh and blood, are no more architects of the world in which we live than are other animals, and certainly, we are less so than the plants and vegetables that first fed the chain of life, as well as that "inanimate" mass that we call Earth and which provides us with the elements we are made of, allowing us to discuss "our" rights.

With the term "environment," I mean everything that exists, and which man does not catalog as animal life, and, therefore, both plants and minerals: we could say that what exists is divided into what has life and what does not have it, but since we do not know what life is or how it is born, we would make the wrong distinctions.

I do not think there is anything "dead" in the universe since at the microscopic level, everything "is alive," meaning it moves and contains energy; on closer inspection, the atoms scattered in space do not just exist and move but combine, constantly exchanging energy and producing new matter, of different shapes and characteristics: they produce life and, even before that, existence, therefore they must, in turn, be life and existence.

Different states of existence correspond to different needs, and therefore different rights: if what lives has the right to live, what exists has the same right to exist.

What could be the rights of the environment? Naturally, we can exclude those that presuppose a conscience or the manifestation of will: unlike animals, we cannot figure self-determination. Nevertheless, the environment has a function and predispositions with which we can interfere.

The maintenance of balance, both at the atomic level and at the level of the galaxies, is allowed by the action of opposing forces, many of which are completely unknown to us or that we find difficult to understand: the Earth is no exception. Every time we interfere with these balances, we commit a transgression, which nature repays with very simple and just sanctions, as dictated exclusively by the principle of balance.

If we were to violate the rights of the environment to the point of destroying the biosphere definitively, we would be the first to suffer the sanction, as proportionally more affected than any other species. Surely the right to exist includes the right to do so in an undisturbed way: if it is normal for every terrestrial person to use the planet's resources, it is also a duty that this happens with respect for the latter.

Environmental rights are higher in plants, given their complexity, greater than what we see in the so-called inanimate matter.

Since life has different complexities, rights should be modulated differently and appropriately: the greater complexity of the tree than the stone determines the emergence of a further right.

If, for example, it is impossible to kill a mineral, it is instead possible to kill a tree.

In addition to recent scientific investigations that suggest pain perception by plants, if they are deprived of water or light, they wither and die, ceasing their organized functions.

If someone or something can be damaged, it is necessary to recognize the right not to be damaged, and therefore the corresponding duty of others to refrain from doing so.

It would be a mistake to consider only the planet Earth as an environment worthy of respect: we must consider it just as part of a much larger universe, wherefrom immensely small to immensely large, there is a connection and a constant exchange.

The Earth would not exist without the Sun, nor, more generally, could matter exist in the forms we know without the action of the stars. But the stars are nothing but an aggregation of matter; therefore, once again, they are what we are and vice versa: a multitude of combinations and transformations that lead to different forms, always starting from the same substance.

A rock or a blade of grass and a human being is different in innumerable profiles and, therefore, they will have different rights in terms of quality and size, but this does not imply that one has and the other does not.

The rock enjoys a right to exist as much as the human being, and any denial of this derives from the use of simple prejudices and will: abstractly, the elimination of that rock could cause more damage to the Earth/universe system than that of a human being, since the latter could be the cause of innumerable damage to the system with which it interacts, while the former could be fundamental for the balance of the elements in a given place, providing hospitality to numerous forms of life or perhaps the very essence of a form of life yet to be developed.

If all the men on Earth decided together to remove or destroy all the rocks they encountered or simply transfer them all to the same place, what would happen? The alteration of equilibrium would cause consequences hard to realize: the same, even if more noticeable, happens with deforestation. Any man has the right to kill (cut) a tree: what if everyone on Earth would cut a tree every day of his life? If we feel this unconceivable, then we understand that there must be a universal principle valid in both cases: from the single individuals to all the humankind.

The effects of deforestation are widely visible and documented by consolidated scientific literature,[21] yet if everyone had the right to indiscriminately dispose of nonsentient beings, on what grounds could it be said that it is wrong/immoral to destroy entire forests?

We will have to determine which and how many rights there are, not "if" there are any.

Today we are already able to destroy our planet, for example, with the use of atomic bombs that would devastate the biosphere, but future technological progress will make us much more dangerous and interfere with even larger balances. For this reason, acquiring the awareness of the rights of everything that exists is fundamental and will become so more and more.

The first step toward this awareness consists in rejecting the instrumental perspective of the environment that has inspired us in our most recent history and which, since the industrial revolution, has compromised the balance of nature with exponential speed.

The juridical conception that has disregarded any rights to subjects other than human beings, then making enormous conceptual efforts to reintroduce them with severe mental disabilities, unborn children, future generations, etc., has rooted in a Western society the idea that it cannot be considered wrong to plunder the environment.

We must be aware that environmental rights must be affirmed in and of itself as an intrinsic value.

The Earth and its elements create our bodies; how could we have more rights than what we come from? But, on the other hand, how could we have absolute rights toward what originated and sustains us?

Without the environment, there is no man, but the environment can exist (no doubt better) without man: who has the most right to hold rights?

In conclusion, the environment has the fundamental right to exist, and, therefore, the resulting right not to be disturbed in its state and development and not to be damaged; the damage criterion must be related to the actual situation regarding each specific entity.

3.5 A UNIFIED THEORY OF THE RIGHT

Like any moral theory that considers only a few groups or individuals, such a limited rights theory can only be erroneous and fallacious.

The key to overcoming the particularities and the numerous uncertainties that have afflicted and continue to afflict jurists and philosophers lies precisely in the ability to synthesize and address all the issues within a single theory.

This theory cannot fail to consider all the inhabitants of the Earth and has to renounce the typical perspective from which lawmakers have always taken steps to date: no theory can be correct if it is rooted in the interests of those who formulated it.

Eusebism is meant to realize an evolution *per saltum*, which to renounce all intermediate steps, undoubtedly superfluous and even harmful, as they are liable to slow down indefinitely the complete implementation of rights.

First, it is necessary to discern between the meaning of right understood as law and that in the sense of just or moral: the first is a practical need, the second is the utopian aspiration (at least in this historical moment).

The current law lies on associates' approval, and, therefore, only if there is an agreement between the parties involved, it makes sense to talk about mutual renunciations and reciprocal rights.

The fact that nonhumans cannot enter the so-called social contract, or execute it in any way, implies that they must remain alien to it: for this reason, our laws cannot interfere with other than human beings.

Every species and group obey the laws that belong to them, which can be written, unwritten, dictated by someone, or imposed by nature, chemistry, or physics.

We should note that humans are not entitled, with their laws, to interfere with different laws, such as nonhuman animal societies in the wild or those that govern the evolution, survival of life, and the biosphere.

Our theories on rights must consider rights different from ours, while a legal system must be limited to the members of the community that invented it.

But what rights must therefore be recognized? Again, morality represents the starting point for identifying individual rights, or, in other words, individuals' rights.

In this case, absolute relativism makes no sense: for example, stating that it is lawful to make laws based on the individuals' or rulers' will is meaningless since this would mean attributing absolute value to something arbitrary. If a whole society endorses genocide, does this become lawful?

The moral principle that identifies right and wrong cannot vary over time or culture and even less from individual to individual. In this case, it will be the concept of evolution that acts as an absolute and immanent reference.

Anything that promotes evolution, considered in the holistic sense of the term, will be morally right; on the contrary, everything that determines an involution must be reproved by the laws.

The essential parameter of evolution is, of course, the pursuit of maximum equilibrium: this is an absolute parameter as it can be relativized; that is, it can be adapted from time to time to each case.

What determines a balance between the interests of the subjects involved can be considered just, whether it is the construction of a power plant to produce energy or a contract; so, the power plant that should be running on timber would not be lawful simply as the right to life of trees must prevail over the interests of humans to use certain electrical tools.

The consequences of applying this principle today can certainly be considered utopian, unworkable, and revolutionary. If you think so, it is probably because you are accustomed to our system; on the other hand, it is a sick and self-destructive system that can never be eliminated except at the root, questioning the very foundation of actions and laws.

Once humanity assumes evolution as a fundament of its moral, it will eventually emancipate itself from the false need of right and laws; this will imply the pursuit of equilibrium as the final goal of each individual.

NOTES

1. Famous is the definition of natural law given by Ulpian and transfused in the Digest of Justinian: "*Natural Law is What Nature Has Taught to All Animated Beings Who Are Born on Land and in the Sea, and Also to Birds*" (Digest, 1, 1, 1, 3).
2. Kant, Immanuel, *The Metaphysics of Morals*, 1797.
3. Rawls, John, *A Theory of Justice*, Oxford, 1971.
4. Ibidem, p. 418.
5. Bekoff, Marc, Pierce, Jessica, *Wild Justice: The Moral Lives of Animals*, The University of Chicago Press, 2009.
6. Brandt, Richard B., *A Theory of the Good and the Right*, Oxford University Press, 1979.
7. Bekoff, Pierce, Ibidem.
8. Ibidem, p. 63.
9. Ibidem, p. 172.
10. Hare, Richard Mervyn, *Pensiero morale* [*Moral Thought*], Il Mulino, Bologna, 1969, p. 57.
11. Asimov, I., Silverberg, R., *Robot NDR-113*, Bompiani, Milan, 1992.
12. Goldberg, Bruce, *Past Lives, Future Lives*, Armenia Editore, Milan, 1992, p. 183.
13. The concept of inferiority/superiority, in this case, is parameterized on the average opinion of human civilization and on the assumption that it has been adopted in relating its laws and rights to all other terrestrials. It is not a certain parameter, nor an absolute one, but its arbitrariness is useful to clarify its limits and inevitable contradictions.
14. *The Arrival of Wang*, Manetti Bros., Iris Film, Italy, 2011.
15. To be more precise, we should affirm *what on the phenomenal level appears other than us*, in consideration of the principle of circularity.

16. Falcòn Y Tella, J. M., Falcòn Y Tella, F., *Fondamento e scopo della pena: diritto di punire?* [*Basis and Purpose of the Sanction: Right to Punish?*], Giuffrè, Milan, 2008, p. 87.

17. Bekoff, Pierce, Ibidem.

18. Bobbio, Norberto, Diritti umani e società [Human Rights and Society], in *Sociologia del diritto* [*Sociology of Law*] 1989, n. 1, p. 25.

19. Ostrander, Elaine, Ruvinsky, Anatoly, *The Genetics of the Dog*, 2nd edition, CPI Group, UK, 2012, p. 1.

20. The term environment is clearly limited and limiting and is not used regarding the established meaning, but as a generic definition of what exists and does not fall into the category of animals: in this sense, it would be incorrect to speak of "plants" or "plant life," But also of "life."

21. Suave, David J., *Effects of Deforestation*, 2013, eBook. Vajpeyi, Dhirendra K., *Deforestation, Environment, and Sustainable Development*, Praeger, 2001.

Chapter 4

Moral

The term moral refers to the judgment on just or unjust underlying specific conducts: moral philosophies aim to determine which actions are right or wrong.

So far, there have been dozens of moral theories, although many simply derive from the main currents around which specific interpretations have developed.

Using words invented by others and largely inflated can be dysfunctional if we decide to start something new and original. In particular, we need to make a clean sweep on various issues, which, speaking of morals, over the centuries have ended up involving thought through a schematization and a notion that has made it more a stance rather than ideation.

4.1 TOWARD A UNIVERSAL MORAL

Questioning life in the universe poses yet another subjective interpretation: what we can observe represents only a part of everything that exists and that in recent decades science has shown to transcend the human senses.

Physics has long been aimed at defining the so-called theory of everything, that is, a law capable of explaining all observable phenomena, from the principle that determines the formation of atomic nuclei (strong force) to what keeps us anchored to the Earth (gravitation), up to quantum mechanics. Philosophy and physics are unequivocally linked and thus coexisted in the works of the ancient Greek philosophers, while they split up during the Middle Ages and rejoined from the Enlightenment.

The philosophical doctrine of physicalism, invented in the twentieth century, attributed absolute value to physics, discarding all knowledge extraneous to it: even this perspective, however, while assuming to start from certain elements (space and time), was denied by the same science that understood relativity with Einstein and that today faces with ever greater conviction the possibility of parallel universes, suggesting that our very existence does not take place within a universe but in a multiverse.[1]

Advances in physics and technology have allowed us to detect innumerable phenomena and energies that we never knew before since they do not fall within that small portion of that which we can learn through our senses.

We can make an example to understand the relativity of our statements. Let us imagine standing in front of a skyscraper at various distances.

i) At 5 inches from it, our perception would be extremely limited, allowing us only to affirm that we are in front of a wall.
ii) At a distance of 10 feet, we would understand that we were not in front of a wall, or, better, that the wall was part of something larger: some of us may already understand that it is a skyscraper, but without being able to see all the sides or where it ends.
iii) At a distance of 30 feet, all of us would have the awareness that the one in front of us is a skyscraper, but we would still have a partial and unbalanced vision: we could perceive the facade facing us and the extension in height, but without having certainty about the shape of the summit, or the overall development.
iv) A few hundred feet away, we could see the absolute consistency of the building, its shape, and its extension: in short, we could describe it correctly. However, our description would be limited only to the outside, not perceiving anything hidden in each of its planes.
v) Entering the skyscraper, we would see how it is structured and what happens inside, and we would thus be aware of the form and its essence. At this point, most of us would be convinced that we have understood every part of the skyscraper, as everything we saw has been explored: some may wonder how the existence of such a work is possible and hypothesizing that there is something that, although invisible, is decisive.
vi) After having developed sufficiently advanced technology, we could verify the theories supported by some and discover the existence of the foundations: only at this point would we have reached an essential knowledge and not limited only to what was visible.

If we relate the example of the skyscraper to our awareness of the Earth, we could consider ourselves in the fourth phase: still unable to explore its real essence and, certainly, unaware of everything that the senses or current technology cannot reveal us.

Physics teaches that the universe (or the multiverse) descends from an event conventionally defined as the Big Bang, that is, a sort of primordial explosion from which what surrounds us was created.[2] The unitary principle theorized by many ancient philosophers was therefore finally found after a few millennia. However, such awareness determines a further reflection: not only human beings and animals have a common root, but everything, animate or inanimate, comes from the same matrix and the same elements.

The conceptual consequences are extraordinary: our sense of belonging has traditionally been built starting from the closest bonds, and, little by little, it has extended toward the most remote ones.

We Are Alike

The hypothesis that similarity or empathy is a source of rights/duties does not seem acceptable: on the other hand, all the disciplines based on these assumptions should today be remeasured, since if it is true that humans descend from monkeys, it is also true that it, like any other form of life, in turn, descends from that primordial soup formed on Earth a few billion years ago and of which it is still difficult to understand the spark of life. The soup, in turn, derives from the elements present on Earth, which originated with the Big Bang.

Philosophical currents are divided between materialism and transcendentalism: some consider only the visible matter, while others consider transcendental.

The whole universe we are immersed in, and that has generated us, derives from a unity, which could be the beginning of everything, or a cyclic event, or the simple product of unknown phenomena originating in parallel universes: in each of these cases, the matrix would be unique and, therefore, any principle of a materialistic nature should consider, both from the point of view of the evolutionary derivation and the point of view of the creator's right over creation, the inseparability of the human position from that of any other element of the universe (or multiverse).

The Greek philosopher Empedocles defined the original unity of the whole as *One* or *Sphere*: something that breaks up and subdivides, creating the universe in a cyclical succession that recalls the Big Bang and the inflationary universe, that is destined to contract until it reaches the unit, only to explode again.[3]

On closer inspection, there are no substantial differences in what we can observe in the universe: from stars to planets, the differences are only formal since atoms and their essential components, quarks, differ only in composition but not in behavior.

Observed at the atomic level, a cell does not differ from a crystal: possessing the ability to manipulate atomic nuclei, it would be possible to produce "living" matter or not and reproduce any phenomenon that has generated life on Earth or in the universe.

From whatever mechanism, principle, will, or phenomenon life is derived, it certainly comes from what is traditionally defined as "nonlife," that is, from the so-called inanimate matter: even religious theories on the origin of human life affirm that man comes from the substance of which the Earth is made.

The root of Adam's name, first used in Judaism and later in Christianity, to indicate the first man, has the meaning of "earth"[4]; in the traditions of these religions, the divinity would have created man from mud, that is, from inanimate matter.

Whether the biological trigger at the base of man originated on Earth or elsewhere, in a cosmic cloud, on a star, or another planet, does not change the fact that the matrix is common and that every "living" being can see the light only through the use and transformation of "nonliving" matter: before birth, anyone experiences a fetal stage during which body is grown through the mother, who is fed on air, water, minerals, salt, and such.

How is it possible to discriminate the "inanimate" matter compared to "animate"? The difference is only apparent and temporary, considering that all the functions attributed to what lives by contemporary biology are destined to cease within a given time, and the animated matter is destined to return inanimate and vice versa, in a continuous succession of state changes. Denying the right to the existence of that primordial soup would be equivalent to removing the foundations of the pyramid where we place man and all his rights at the top. From all the above derive consequences that some might consider revolutionary, but simply represent the logical corollary of the impartial observation of what, so far, the human being has managed to know about what surrounds it.

We can analyze reality on different scales: from the subatomic to the cosmic level; in any case, humans have only an awareness, limited to current technology.

Of course, planet Earth itself does not possess the attributes of life as it is defined in biology. Yet, it is a complex system that, seen as a whole, regulates itself, can maintain itself, evolve, modify itself, and even repair itself: all its components (except man) interact profitably with each other, contributing to the proper functioning of the system.

Can we compare the human body and the Earth? If you cut the skin with a knife, this wound bleeds, then the blood solidifies, seals the opening, and soon new cells fill the spaces between the edges of the lesion, creating the skin again. Likewise, if you make an asphalt road on a lawn and then abandon it without any maintenance: the rain, the wind, the frost, and the sun, in their succession, would create cracks in that strip of asphalt, where plants would be born and grow, widening the cracks and slowly crumbling the road, of which in the end there would be no trace.

A single cell among those involved in the skin regeneration process after cutting is not very different from the blade of grass or the tree that creeps between the cracks in the asphalt. Yet, no one would deny the person to whom those cells belong is injured, although no one recognizes the sentient nature of the cells, nor the ownership of rights: in short, it does not seem necessary to prove that each plant or mineral is the holder of rights, to affirm that it is worthy of protection and respect.

Even starting from the anthropocentric point of view, which is the opposite of the one just examined, one faces the same conclusions: since every rock, every tree, every stream, and every blade of grass participate in the equilibrium that is at the base of the system on which human beings themselves depend, the contempt of the former automatically determines the damage to the latter and their rights.

Equality in Diversity

The principle of equality often used to claim a right to equal treatment is not reflected in nature and even risks annihilating the values underlying relationships: the fact that only "equal" individuals can enjoy equal rights or make the same claims is a false premise since it is a prejudiced criterion.

True equity is not achieved through the affirmation of equality that often does not exist but through the explicit recognition of specific needs and characteristics. Therefore, we must avoid and reject homologation and ensure that, even in diversity, each can realize himself, according to the ends and the modalities that he or nature has established.

Over the last centuries, philosophers who cared about animals have tried to show that they think, suffer, and feel like us, but this is not at all necessary: there are people who, by birth or because of accidents, have lost the use and sensitivity of limbs or whole parts of their body, but no one feels (or is) entitled to remove these parts, to injure them, or to dispose of them for food, to entertain themselves or to carry out experiments.

If suffering were the basis of the rights/duties, the above should be allowed, but it is not, since we recognize that everyone enjoys a sphere of autonomy and self-determination that others' claims cannot invade. This is regardless of external evaluations about the opportunity, need, or harmfulness.

Of course, none of us would ever accept to sacrifice himself for the protection of rock and, consequently, we try to morally justify what an innate instinct represents: we choose every day to use several entities (animate/inanimate), and our conscience suggests that we consider all this available, since otherwise, we would have to begin feeling responsible for these immense abuses.

There is a fundamental distinction between doing something because we like it and doing it because we think it is right, but we are naturally induced to affirm that everything we do is right, while without hesitation, we define unfair what we want to avoid doing/undergo.

Establishing what is right presupposes the adoption of a criterion to which we relate our actions from time to time: this criterion must be impartial, objective, and absolute since otherwise, it would end up becoming the mere justification for the action mentioned above. Thus, for example, you can decide to move or even destroy a stone, and the stone cannot oppose it, much less does any legal rule prohibit it: can we, therefore, consider this action "right"?

The large-scale application of a criterion, taking it to its extreme consequences, demonstrates its limits and contradictions: what is universally right must be practicable by anyone for an unlimited number of times, but if this is not possible, it means that it is not even fair. Often, we confuse what "we can do" with what we "have the right to do," assuming that what is possible to us is also right or morally correct.

Expand Awareness

We should figure a new moral system, which is disconnected from the speculations, sometimes revolutionary, of modern and contemporary philosophy and which, by recovering the genes of the older one, dissolves the chains that have bound it to the unilateral perspective of the human observer, of its possibilities, knowledge, and resources.

We extend our considerations from what we know (or think we know) to everything we imagine (or do not imagine) in search of universal criteria whose formulation cannot in any way betray their origin: the principles of such a moral should be unnoticeable, should it come from man, a dog, a worm or even a Martian.

Only by removing at the base any vice capable of giving rise to prejudices, particularisms, opportunisms, and favoritisms we can, then, proceed in the search for the universally right, rather than the right "here, now, for me."

The main requirements that a universal moral system must possess are the following:

1) It cannot be based a priori on the needs or perspectives of those who formulate it.
2) It cannot have the purpose of justifying conduct put in place by those who formulate it.

3) It must be relativized to rise to an absolute value.[5]
4) It must distinguish principles from actions and provide for different levels of virtuosity.
5) It must be adaptable to imperfection, characteristic of sensitive reality; the least possible evil must be considered the objective immediately subordinate to the good.
6) Theoretical moral must be distinguished from practical moral based on intentions rather than effects.

So, what is the principle we should adopt toward everything that surrounds us, even before asking ourselves whether it is alive, suffers, understands, resembles us, or not?

Removing an entity from what it is spontaneously or deliberately assigned represents an interference that will have consequences both on the entity itself and on everything that enters or will enter into a relationship with it.

The above also reflects the principle of correlation of rights: protecting the rights of a being implies protecting all beings that depend on it and are related to it.

The correlation principle operates in both directions: you cannot, for example, protect animals if you do not protect the environment, and therefore it is not even possible to safeguard the first and not the second.

Conduct consisting of abuse understood as overexploitation of resources is inevitably immoral and therefore censurable, meaning any form of exploitation incompatible with their existence/persistence.

Based on the above, many claim the right of human beings to pursue happiness and, therefore, conclude that other moral instances, especially when referring to beings of another nature, are subordinate.

Also, in this case, we need to question the very roots: could we really consider happiness as a moral instance or the goal of our lives?

If endorsed by current law, the pursuit of individual happiness must always be balanced by providing the limit represented by the right of others or the pursuit of happiness: it is not an absolute parameter that can determine what is absolutely right or wrong.

Furthermore, it is not possible to affirm that the pursuit of one's happiness is right even for the individual himself: this interior condition, variously interpreted by each one, can also reside in a state of self-destruction such as those deriving from the excessive intake of psychotropic substances or food, and such.

Both moral and current law can and must be inspired not by the mere pursuit of happiness, but by the fulfillment of the individuals' expectations, ensuring that everyone enjoys the same conditions to succeed, and, above all, by removing the obstacles and barriers that discriminate based on to the belonging of species, race, sex, and such.

All utilitarian theories are superficially liable to direct toward correct behavior, but they are wrong when considering the pursuit of happiness as a parameter of just or unjust. First, the idea of happiness is different for everybody; moreover, the utilitarian proposition "maximum benefit for the greatest number of individuals" could certainly justify the persecutions perpetrated in every time over the history against minorities.

Once again, there is the risk of falling into subjective, absolute relativism: it is no coincidence that the "philosophy" of pursuing pleasure and fulfillment is the basis of most contemporary Western society's problems.

The only absolute principle to which a system of moral can strive is not vacuous (and subjective, therefore indefinable a priori) well-being, but—rather—self-realization and evolution: these last two criteria can well be parameterized based on equilibrium, understood as the ability of each to interact constructively with what surrounds him, without harming himself or others.

There can be no moral value in behaviors that are not oriented to evolve and realize equilibrium (inside and outside of oneself) since an existence exclusively devoted to maximizing one's benefit is an end in itself and is incompatible with others' rights.

In and of itself, the pursuit of one's happiness is morally irrelevant: only if it is parameterized to the interests of everything that surrounds us can it also conform to moral, while, otherwise, it could indifferently be neutral or even immoral. Moreover, history and science have shown increasing evidence of how particularisms represent simple, functional diversifications unsuitable for establishing real distinctions in rights.

A human being who loses the ability to understand, being in a condition of neurovegetative coma, is not considered a mere thing, nor ceases to be a rightsholder. Therefore, we cannot explain the source of the rights through moral doctrines based on the intellectual faculty or individuals' attitude to suffering.

It is no coincidence that a disabled person is usually defined as "a vegetable," since he has lost all those faculties of interaction characteristic of animal life despite maintaining basic vital functions. Therefore, we should assume that denying rights to plants results in denying to disabled persons as well.

I am not suggesting denying rights to disabled people (!): we should extend them to plants, to avoid inconsistent conclusions.

Objective and Subjective Moral

Historically, it is controversial whether an absolute moral system could exist or not.

It is a fact that each person has moral: everyone acts and intends right based on different values, and, from time to time, the conclusions can be opposite. But the fact that something happens does not automatically imply that it is right: if everyone thinks he is right, we can see that he can be wrong as well.

When we talk about the origin of the universe, for example, numerous different hypotheses are opposed, which, dividing into currents, in turn, have ramifications: can we perhaps conclude that the universe has had as many origins as there are theories? No. In the same way, the plurality of moral theories (or ideas) does not invalidate the existence of a single moral.

On the other hand, individual moral is based on a mixture of suggestions, beliefs, conditioning, and perspectives that are not objective: an absolute principle must be both outside and above everything, having to relate indiscriminately with any of those elements without being influenced.

The purpose of Eusebism is to describe absolute morals.

Eusebist moral is empirical because it is based on observation, limiting logical operations to a minimum.

Each mental passage represents a complication, therefore a risk of error and sophistication of the truth and the possibility of contamination with prejudice or a subjective perspective, which would distort the results: it is fundamental that objective moral contains only the essential.

By falling into relativism, murder and torture could be justified, while saving someone's life would be questionable.

In this case, the result is opposite to the previous one; in fact, it must be denied that there is a plurality of subjective morals, concluding that moral is one and it has to be objective.

We may be unable to find the absolute principle of moral, but this does not affect its existence in any way.

We can approach the matter using hermeneutics: removing subjective ideas from moral, what remains has to be objective.

Equilibrium is undoubtedly the ideal parameter to find objective morals.

The best method to ensure that the objectification operation is successful is to approach the issues from a global perspective and as technical as possible (in the sense of nonevaluative).

If, for example, in a place where we had decided to dig into cultivating a plant, we found an anthill, any human solution that concluded for the destruction of the anthill would be biased and based on discrimination, that is, that the ants are less important than human beings.

Again, if we recognize the right of an individual to cut a plant, we should recognize the right of any individual to cut any plant and so abstractly the right that any human can eliminate the entire vegetation of the planet: the outcome would be harmful if not lethal.

4.2 MORAL AGENTS AND PATIENTS

Moral philosophy is used to distinguish between agents and patients: the former are those subjects considered capable of acting morally oriented, while the latter can suffer the effects of others' actions but not act according to morality.

Human beings are—of course—agents, although there are some exceptions: the newborns, disabled, and, in general, all the subjects who, for congenital or accidental reasons, lack mental faculties considered necessary for moral evaluations.

The most elementary and even intuitive conclusion is that only moral agents are bearers of interests worthy of being recognized through actual rights. In contrast, moral patients would be disposable as they are unable to assume duties and understand the moral significance of their actions.

The classic formulation of the agents/patients dyad, therefore, contemplates normal adult human subjects on the one hand (moral agents), and all the other animals on the other side (moral patients): in this scheme, only the former would be bearers of rights and duties as considered suitable for this.

Philosophers such as Singer and Regan, while starting from different assumptions, concluded the same: we should take into account the interests of moral patients.

Bentham, who attributed importance to suffering, discerning it from the ability to speak, is fundamental to recognize moral relevance to moral patients.

In my opinion, the above said theories fail in practice: who determines who can act in a morally oriented sense? It depends exclusively on the observer and his ability to understand the surrounding reality: see, for example, the description of the subjects-of-a-life made by Regan, which rests on such arbitrary bases that he defines it as merely indicative, conventional, and nonexhaustive.[6]

There cannot be a line to demarcate the boundary between moral agents and patients. Therefore, the two categories cannot exist either: instead, there is an infinite series of shades of awareness, and therefore of interpretation and understanding of the effects of their conduct, as well as adapting to them.

For example, a five-year-old human may not be aware of his rights and duties, but this does not imply that he does not have his moral conception and does not comply with it.

Usually, when we state that someone is capable of moral judgments and someone else is not, we affirm something relative: we could not evaluate others' attitude to operate according to morals, in general, but only according to our morals.

Not knowing or not understanding moral evaluations different from ours, or at least based on different parameters and expressions, it is impossible or extremely difficult to determine who is or is not a moral agent.

The studies of Pierce and Bekoff have shown unequivocally how nonhuman subjects possess expectations and can recognize those of others, working from time to time to meet their own needs or those of others, possibly enduring sacrifices for the good of those who are other than themselves. In short, dividing categories is wrong, but is it, at least, useful?

If the interests of all subjects—be they, agents or patients—deserve equal consideration, then what is the point of dividing them? This could only be useful to discriminate: one side is better than the other side.

There are no moral agents or patients, except in the eye of those who want to see them: anyone acts in the way, for the purposes and based on the assumptions that belong to him, based on evaluations that from the outside may seem meaningful and relevant, as well as completely ludicrous and unmotivated.

In conclusion, I believe that this classification also represents an unnecessary obstacle to understanding the relationship with the other by oneself, and therefore it is not appropriate to perpetuate it, as it is the result of determinism and prejudice.

4.3 PEOPLE, ALMOST PEOPLE, AND NONPEOPLE

A person is generally identified as that subject capable of certain specific thoughts or acts, including expressing a will and performing particular actions.[7]

In the history of thought, there has been a succession of interpretations of the concept of person, which have extended or limited its recognizability based on different parameters: Singer's thought was considered revolutionary, as he excluded some human beings from the concept of per, including nonhumans (or some of them).[8]

Beyond the brilliant, albeit abstract, considerations about the aptitude to be considered a person, it is clear that the aim (or at least the relapse) is to establish once again who is the recipient of rights and duties: it is usual to discuss such issues in the bioethics debate.[9]

From a philosophical perspective, the person is exactly the citizen in the legal sphere and, indeed, perhaps even more: the legislator himself.

Our society is governed by normally developed adult human beings: laws and philosophies, even trying to expand rightsholders, never abandoned their own perspective. The male legislator, white and wealthy, enslaved African people and limited women's and poor people's rights.

What is the need to determine who or what a person is, apart from justifying the exploitation of whom is not considered a person?

Suppose there could ever be a pure and disinterested purpose in designating this category. In that case, it should be a merely descriptive operation, which, in order not to be fallacious, should be based on objective circumstances: parameters such as self-awareness or the representation of reality, in how completely unknowable from the outside, cannot be considered as such.

The scientific attempts to limit the possession of certain intellectual faculties, to which the title of person can be traced, are not only undermined by the lack of scientific knowledge on which they relate, but are also erroneous as it is not sufficient to demonstrate that there is a difference to link discrimination to it.

The problem, therefore, is not to establish who is a person and who is not, but whether this completely arbitrary definition has any use or at least the possibility of describing something existing rather than creating it.

Instead of inventing new criteria to establish the exploiters and the exploited, it would be far more desirable to understand the others through merely descriptive operations, to guarantee the pursuit of equilibrium.

Until now, we have used a binary and digital concept of person/nonperson, while I strongly recommend making an analogical analysis, which looks more suitable to the infinite variety of beings and variables of existence.

4.4 THEORETICAL MORAL

Premises

An action can be subjectively moral but objectively immoral: for example, a sailor could throw a life vest at a drowning person, hitting him in the face and killing him. No doubt that he acted in good faith, but the consequence is nefarious and the cause of damage.[10] In this case, based on its effects, the action was commendable, but based on the intentions, it was right.

We can distinguish between a theoretical moral, "of intentions," and a practical moral, "of effects": a compartmentalized system, such as those that consider only the agent's intentions, would be fallacious and would lack the complexity of the actions.

Only taking into account the two distinct aspects, or the different points of view, we can resolve the dichotomy between intentions and results of the life jacket example: to examine the affair only based on the effects would mean condemning someone who did not act "against moral," while, conversely, taking into account only the intentions would end up approving a fact that is harmful in itself.

In this sense, the theoretical/practical distinction is particularly relevant, even fundamental, in law and in the philosophy of law, disciplines aimed at sanctioning the limits of actions, not so much based on intentions, but of their substantial effects.

What is the relation between theoretical and practical morals? They are independent. The agent can be wrong and his action harmful, while he is in good faith.

Only the inversion of the perspective can allow a theoretically correct and abstractly universal approach: anything that exists must enjoy rights unless their exercise is harmful to the rights of others.

Classification

It is possible to schematize the value/disvalue of pure moral as follows:

−3: thoughts aimed at others' damage or injury
−2: actions aimed at others' damage or injury
−1: omissions aimed at others' damage or injury
0: omissions of actions aimed at others' damage or injury
+1: abstention from omissions aimed at others' damage or injury
+2: actions aimed at the benefit of others
+3: thoughts aimed at others' benefit

For example, in this scheme, veg(etari)anism is placed at level 0 because we cannot consider it an option, nor a supererogatory behavior, but rather a duty.

If it is true that no one who feeds on animals can claim to love them, it is not only those who intend to act for their good which will have to consider vegetarianism a moral imperative: refraining from killing them is not a benevolent, loving, or generous action, but simply the fulfillment of a duty.

Therefore, it would be appropriate to overcome the "vegetarianism = animal advocacy" paradigm: on the other hand, no one has ever claimed that a human being is a philanthropist just because he fails to eat human beings. Animal advocacy cannot exist without vegetarianism, but the latter can exist without the first, since eating animal derivatives is placed at the −3 level of the moral scale and does not represent a right for anyone.

Relations with the Law

The ascertainment of intentions, characteristic of theoretical moral, is also relevant for imposing the sanction: in manslaughter, for example, punishments are different based on whether it is willful or unintentional.

The principle of "guilt" codified by law cannot correspond to moral, since otherwise, it would end up attributing relevance to artificial categories: it can be argued that a driver driving his car at 40 mph is legally guilty of having run over a pedestrian, but from a moral point of view there is no analogy.

Theoretical moral must take into consideration exclusively the intentions and disposition of the mind of the agent. At the same time, the judgment of positive law cannot ignore the effects (practical moral): the understanding of the real intentions of the agent is often precluded to the external observer, daily coexistence must be based on precepts that consider the effects and impose the appropriate sanctions to avert them.

The current law does not completely disregard the so-called pure moral and provides mitigating and aggravating parameters based on intentions/ motivations.

Practical moral translates the idealism of pure moral into the pragmatism of daily action: these are those behaviors that, in the impossibility of adhering to pure dictates, are nevertheless inspired as much as possible by them.

We commonly say that the law cannot judge the intentions, thus meaning that people can be prosecuted because of their actions, not because of their thoughts. This does not mean that the law cannot consider moral issues at all: they cannot be considered separately from the conduct: in the case of murder, the investigation aimed at ascertaining whether the agent intended to cause death or not will determine the type of crime and, possibly, its very existence.

4.5 PRACTICAL MORAL

Premises

The effects assume moral relevance to the extent that they participate in determining the agent's will. Thus, for example, if you want to kill a person and you kill him, the moral evaluation based on the consequences is correct; not so if the agent wanted to save a person who was accidentally killed: in this case, the effects would not be consistent with the will, and a moral condemnation would be wrongful.

Theoretical moral is often not suitable to everyday life: we can, therefore, consider practical moral as the interface between idealism and pragmatism. When it is impossible to adhere to theoretical moral, practical moral leads to a median path that causes less damage. We cannot say "the least possible damage," since otherwise with this definition, we would return to pure moral: it is not technically impossible to refrain from damage, but often it is simply complicated or would involve changes deemed too drastic: we must therefore return to a variable and not an absolute parameter, which requires constant comparison, in search of the best compromise.

Practical moral must not and cannot substitute pure moral, since—otherwise—from a mere transitory parameter, it would be self-referential, therefore completely irrelevant. If a pure moral precept requires facing the issues from an eminently (if not exclusively) qualitative point of view, then practical moral, assuming that the precepts of pure moral are not fully applied, will minimize the effects from a pure moral precept quantitative point of view.

If, for example, it is possible to choose between purchasing two different products, of which the first caused pollution equal to 100 and the second equal to 50, the practical moral imposes to prefer the purchase of the second. At the same time, the theoretical moral will maintain that it is not a correct action, but simply less wrong: not something to be promoted as the desirable action, but practical action to be implemented if—for whatever reason—the precept of pure moral is not fulfillable.

In conclusion, practical moral must be considered as something temporary, that is makeshift, while at the same time inducing us to understand that there is almost always room for improvement, rather than being satisfied, feeling that one has "arrived" only because they have partially changed.

From Digital Moral to Analogical Moral

Moral theories are "binary": on or off, all or nothing, right or wrong. There are no middle ground nor grey areas: resulting precepts are too absolute to be matched and unsuitable for guiding actions. It is not enough to affirm that an action is morally just or unjust since, in concrete action, it is also necessary to determine the amount of justice or injustice underlying it, to prefer the more correct (or less wrong) action: for this reason, it is necessary to overcome the binary concept of moral, in favor of an analogical approach,[11] capable of adapting to social and individual complexities. An example of practical analogical moral can be seen in feeding pets: this represents a considerable problem for ethical vegetarians, forced to endorse the slaughtering industry because—at least in felines—animal food is indispensable, except for the use of supplements.

The morally oriented solution imposes to consider the distortion of the feeding of domestic animals as a lesser evil, compared to the killing (as usual, however, the result of a chain of exploitation and suffering) of breeding animals: likewise, this diet, although not natural, represents a lesser evil than death by starvation or other causes deriving from human interference with the environment and nature.

Suppose the above must be done in observance of practical moral. In that case, however, pure moral requires that the best solution be made possible, that is, one that also respects the principle of self-determination of domestic animals: this can only be achieved by recreating natural habitats without that human manipulation which has precluded them from obtaining nourishment, protection, and freedom.

We can conclude that conduct, not perfect based on pure moral, is nevertheless desirable compared to completely unjust conduct through practical moral. Thus, for example, many criticize vegetarians for not respecting plants: we can harm plants and animals as well, but we should prefer to cause the least harm possible.

Classification

It can be said that an action/omission is "right" as it can determine positive consequences at one or more levels: for example, it is right to treat an injured individual, but would it therefore be possible to define the opposite action as unjust or as an omission? In short, it may well be said that causing injury to others is morally unjust, but is it also possible to affirm that failing to treat a wound represents unjust conduct?

Refraining from remedying damage that has not been caused means acting in a morally neutral manner, since if on the one hand nothing positive is accomplished, on the other hand, one has refrained from doing anything negative.

We can therefore develop a first, essential, system of moral reference for actions/omissions, structured as follows:

– 1 causation of damage
0 noncausation of damage/noncausation of benefit
+ 1 causation of benefit

Level −1 are moral duties, and they should correspond to legal duties; level 0 belongs to all those conducts that are neither to be encouraged nor to be repressed, in which the free self-determination of each is expressed, without this conflicting with the other's right.

Morally commendable and desirable conducts are at level +1, but the omission cannot lead to reprobation or be legally sanctioned. Moral shuns determinism: we often try to distinguish what is right from what is wrong and what is moral from what is immoral, but responsibility (both moral and legal) is not comparable to a binary digital system, which only knows the "on" or "off" options, but rather the analog one, which reproduces all the nuances present between the extremes. The moral classification of conducts in the same way as the principles set out above is the following:

−1: actions/omissions harmful to others
0: omission of actions harmful to others

+1: actions beneficial to others

Disvalue, in the first case, is obvious: for example, hitting a pedestrian while driving is objectively harmful to the pedestrian, therefore reprehensible at most from the point of view of the effects, since the agent, through an act of interference, causes a prejudice that would not have occurred without his action.

On the other hand, the conduct of the agent who merely does not cause harm/benefit does not assume morally positive or negative connotations but remains neutral: if the driver did not run over the pedestrian, this, as compliance with a specific duty (not to harm), would not be per se worthy, but neither could it be considered reprehensible. In the same way, the fact that a passerby, seeing the person hit by the car, does not help him is (morally) neutral, since—beyond current law—a duty to produce a benefit is not recognizable, since this must rather be configured like the real ultimate ambition of the moral system, and therefore a spontaneous act endowed with positive value.

Last, some actions determine a benefit: since the fact of helping others cannot be considered a duty and is clearly not negative, nor neutral; in this case, the agent performs a correct action (from the perspective of the effects), resulting in an improvement in favor of the recipient. Therefore, the fact that the driver stops to help the injured person does not rise to level +1.

Therefore, we can conclude that, while refraining from causing damage constitutes a duty, and as such is coercible, the action aimed at determining a benefit does not configure any duty, but rather the practical moral value to aim for by taking suitable actions and to bring benefits to those who are recipients of their help.

4.6 THE INVISIBLE BOUNDARIES OF GOOD AND EVIL

The fundamental dilemma faced in philosophy is what good is: we can agree that it is not the mere absence of pain. If it were not so, we could impose our will on others when this does not imply any suffering, even if it implies limiting freedom or self-determination.

Happiness, as well, does not seem a sufficient parameter to guarantee the subsistence of the good: it is, in fact, possible, for example, to seek self-destructive experiences and enjoy them without this leading to any real well-being.

We need to distinguish between objective good, which determines an effective benefit, and subjective good, which—vice versa—is what is believed to determine a benefit, but in practice, it is liable to cause harm.

According to pure moral, any motivation placed at the basis of actions based on the joint principles of respect, balance, noninterference, possibility, and circularity should be considered good.

According to practical morality, the good can be determined as the conduct that is most respectful of the greatest number of individuals and, at the same time, harmful to the least number of rights.

In dealing with animals or other beings, we use a "corrective" moral parameter, which transforms conduct from illegal to lawful based on the recipient of the offense or damage. In other words, man does not distinguish good from evil in itself, but attributes a negative value to certain actions only if they affect humans or their interests.

The man himself determines who/what may be rightsholder and, consequently.

Many animal advocates or environmental philosophers tried to prove that animals or the environment has rights and that, therefore, men are required to recognize and respect them. However, I think that no man has ever justified the human right to dispose of everything that is not human.

Furthermore, no one has even ever demonstrated that diversity is a sufficient element to determine the right to dispose of the other (the different) or consider it inferior and treat it as such.

Some talk about *Gaia*, referring to the Earth, personifying it, and attributing it vital characteristics that would make it equal to any other form of life. However, we can see many differences between a "rock" (such as the Moon) and the Earth; this is more than enough to consider the difference between a planet as a home for life forms or life itself.

Considering the objective limitation in our understanding of the surrounding phenomena and discarding the analytical-deterministic criteria for formulating moral precepts, we will have to resort to open models, removing any prejudice or false premise.

In defining universal moral, it is not necessary or possible to foresee all potential behaviors, present or future: only a few elementary principles are necessary and sufficient for this purpose, leading all situations—hypothetical or real—to essential choices.

The difference between one choice and the other is based on a quantitative rather than qualitative criterion: for example, once it is established that what causes suffering is wrong, we can decide not to cause any suffering or, if it is unavoidable to cause suffering, we will be able to choose, considering it right, the option capable of causing the least possible suffering.

But the identification between good and nonsuffering would be reductive, presupposing moreover a further investigation aimed at ascertaining what suffering is; nor can the satisfaction of essential needs be identified with happiness and good, since an action can be harmful even for the person who performs it and, at the same time, guarantee happiness or the realization of expectations. In truth, the number of imaginable situations is so extensive that it is impossible to define a specific conduct a priori as good/right or bad/injurious.

The statement "lying is wrong" might describe a seemingly universal principle, but it is not: would it be right to refer to a person deemed ugly as such? Would it be reprehensible for an atheist to reassure a believer in despair over losing a loved one that he or she is in a better place? There are, in short, situations in which absolute and a priori principles, typical of pure morality, must be combined with contingent and relative principles closer to practical moral.

The cornerstones of the moral system of Eusebism are five:

1) RESPECT (respect the existence of what is other than oneself)
2) BALANCE (the interests involved must be mutually satisfied)
3) NONINTERFERENCE (one should not interfere with the existence, evolution, or survival of that which is other than oneself)
4) POSSIBILITY (repeatability by *n* subjects)
5) CIRCULARITY (the first principle of thermodynamics and Lavoisier's law, nothing is created, nothing is destroyed: everything is transformed).

In conclusion, Eusebism represents the overcoming and, at the same time, the sublimation of all anthropocentric, animalist, environmentalist, or biocentric philosophies. It imposes a form of a priori respect for everything and everyone, to be parameterized from time to time according to each subject taken into consideration.

In any case, the founding principle is that respect is due unless it is proved otherwise.

The pure morality underlying Eusebianism requires that we strive to achieve balance, using altruism as a polar star and renouncing any privilege in the name of similarity, proximity, affection, and such.

Practical moral implies comparing the intentions and the effects of acting, obliging to abstain from those behaviors that would have harmful practical consequences, although ideally conforming to a pure moral.

The fundamental certainty of Eusebism resides in the uncertainty of human knowledge.

We cannot base moral on classifications or distinctions of what exists, still being unable to know and understand fundamental phenomena such as life or its origin, the nature (physical/metaphysical) of what surrounds us, as well as the possible purpose (or randomness) of everything. However, the day our knowledge will be limitless, we could use classifications, even if many arguments suggest avoiding it at all.

In practice, before engaging in any conduct, the Eusebist will ask himself:

1) Is this conduct liable to damage something that exists?
YES → IMMORAL
NO ↓
2) Does it respect the equilibrium?
NO → IMMORAL
YES ↓
3) Does it interfere with others?
YES → IMMORAL
NO ↓
4) Is it possible (repeatable by *n* subjects)?
NO → IMMORAL
YES ↓
5) Does it respect the principle of circularity?
NO → IMMORAL
YES ↓
MORAL

The principles of circularity and noninterference, rather than discriminating, will act as guiding criteria for acting, even as they lack the character of absolutes. For example, it is impossible to say that interference is immoral since it can be interfered with to restore a condition derived from a previous interference. We should strive to redefine our concept of good and evil and avoid cloaking ourselves in that aura of absolute righteousness and justice that often leads us to consider others as tools given ends that we know are superordinate.

It is hard to say if there are absolute good and evil because words have to be interpreted and misunderstood: before answering, we should determine good and evil.

Gaining awareness is an absolute good. From this perspective, the utilitarian principle of well-being does not find any confirmation, given that entertainment can be harmful to those who practice it and those who suffer it while increasing the level of happiness of one or more individuals.

We cannot say that something is good or bad in and of itself, but any circumstance must be subjected to the scrutiny described above to conclude.

Universality means that such a procedure can be used indiscriminately always, in any case, toward anything/anyone. It is, of course, a complex procedure, not immediate, as it requires taking into account different instances. It would be much easier to use a sort of commandment as a rule of action: if I say "do not kill," I know that killing is bad, while not doing it is good. However, commandments lack universality, being limited to issuing a command concerning a precise and unique circumstance; it does not provide any principle to understand what is good or bad in general contexts.

Our effort to understand must go beyond the trivializations and schematisms of thought that have accustomed us to receiving instructions on *what* to think rather than formulating useful reflections for understanding *how* to think. Human actions are complex, as are daily interactions: any thought that omits these elements or does not take them into due consideration, trying to offer simple answers to complex problems, must be rejected a priori.

In conclusion, it is necessary to be ready and willing to question the stereotyped and simplified perspective of good and evil, striving to identify more general, therefore universal, rules and apply them in everyday life, renouncing labels.

4.7 AWARENESS AND MORAL GOOD

If I had to say what without any doubt is moral, I would answer: what determines awareness. Conversely, everything that limits awareness is to be considered immoral.

We commonly consider "evils" the most common result of lack of awareness, and it would therefore be shortsighted and reductive to focus on these, which are mere symptoms, leaving out the real cause: higher levels of awareness lead to "better" behaviors.

Murder is generally considered the most harmful act committed: we reproach those who commit it, while the issue is not the action itself, but the thought that produces it.

Moral's final goal cannot be to eradicate the will to kill: it must be the achievement of the true awareness that murder can never represent a good, not even for those who carry it out.

Who kills, whether by sudden motion (e.g., manslaughter) or premeditated, does that to take advantage: maybe revenge or profit, and such; in any of these cases, the idea of advantage is a false prospect formed in the perception of the agent.

In the first place, there are no killers available to be willingly killed by others: such behavior is based on hypocrisy, and it infringes the principle of equilibrium.

Who kills under the influence of "passionate" instincts does it because he is unable to overcome an inner conflict, for example, for the desire of possession of the other person, or to avenge a wrong (or presumed to be such): in these cases, the agent is a victim, even a prisoner, of his thought. But "liberation" from a torment determined by one's mind can never occur through "the other," and it is, therefore, illusory to persuade oneself otherwise.

Also in the case of homicide for money, there is a lack of awareness: in this case, the agent considers money a good, superior to the others' interest to live or not suffer.

In short, in any case, the murderer, with his act, contributes to making the society in which he participates a deplorable place even based on his own expectations, that is unbalanced, lacking correspondence, and therefore of any kind of respect: the lack of representation of such consequences, that is the absence of awareness, is the real issue to be addressed.

The keystone of the moral system is extremely simple: it is necessary to become aware that harming oneself or others never determines real benefits for the agent and that, therefore, the only moral actions are those that are beneficial for oneself and others. We must parameterize the benefit on intentions (to want good for good's sake) and results (to cause a benefit).

Although we are all endowed with free will, and perhaps indeed for this very reason, only we can be our own jailers, through all the false representations that prevent us from gaining true freedom, that is, the one based on correct information and knowledge of the causes and implications of things and actions.

4.8 MANIFESTO OF THOUGHT

By linking all of the above concepts together, a code of conduct can be outlined, based on the recognition of human, animal, the environment, and everything else that exists.

1. All living things have the right to exist and access the resources necessary for their sustenance.
2. Each animal species and its members have the right to self-determination and the pursuit of happiness and well-being, with mutual respect, unless this limits the equal rights of other living beings.
3. No species has the right to suppress the rights to existence, access to resources, and self-determination of other species.
4. As the top of the terrestrial biological chain, the human species is responsible for its actions and their repercussions toward its members and other species.
5. Any dispositive act by humans toward other species, animals or vegetables, must be limited to rebalancing situations compromised by human intervention.
6. Plants have their dignity, and any disposal by man must respect their nature, without altering it, and be limited to need.

7. In their original conformation and nature, the Earth, the skies, and the seas must be respected and safeguarded, both for themselves and for the forms of life they host and protect.
8. In no case, direct or indirect economic interest can be placed before the rights outlined in points 1 and 2.
9. Any use of resources must be in accordance with the principles, to be applied jointly, of necessity, imperative, expediency, economy, and efficiency.

NOTES

1. Davies, Paul, *A Cosmic Fortune. Life in the Universe: Coincidence or Divine Project?* Mondadori, Milan, 2007, pp. 240, regarding the multiverse, Davies points out that our universe can be a fragment of an immense (probably infinite) and heterogeneous system called the multiverse. The other "universes," or cosmic regions, may be inaccessible to us at the observational level. Their existence would be deduced from theory and from some indirect evidence. The laws of physics and the initial state of the universe could vary from one "universe" to another. What we have interpreted as absolute laws may be more like local laws.

2. Hawking, Stephen, *Dal Big Bang ai buchi neri – Una breve storia del tempo* [*From the Big Bang to Black Holes – A Short History of Time*], Rizzoli, Milan, 1988.

3. Reale, Giovanni, *Invitation to Ancient Thought*, La Scuola Publishing, Brescia, 2011, pp. 46–47.

4. Scquizzato, Paolo, *As a Principle – Reflections on the Book of Genesis*, Effatà Editrice, Turin, 2010, p. 8.

5. It must, in other words, take into consideration each element in its specificity, recognizing its peculiarities and taking them into account.

6. Regan, Tom, *Empty Cages – The Challenge of Animal Rights*, Sonda, Casale Monferrato (AL), 2005, p. 101.

7. The very origin of the term *persona* is lost in history: it is generally traced back to the Greek πρόσωπον and to the Latin persona, understood as a theatrical mask worn by the actors. Starting from stoicism, this word was introduced into philosophical use: with this definition, the stoic Panezio intended to distinguish the human being as a complex entity, distinguished first of all by a mask common to all individuals, but also by that typical of his own character, and that formed during the experiences, and, lastly, from that of his working life. Just after the collapse of the Roman Empire, the thinker Boethius defined a person as "*naturae rationabilis individua substantia*" (individual substance with a rational nature). Over the course of history, the definition has come to coincide with the human being, although not necessarily with any human being: it is still debated whether fetuses, infants, the incapable, some categories of disabled people, etc. can be considered persons. For further information, see Carrithers, M., Collins, S., Lukes, S., *The Category of the Person, Anthropology, Philosophy, History*, Cambridge University Press, UK, 1985.

8. Singer, Peter, *Practical Ethics*, Cambridge University Press, 4th edition, 2011, p. 74.

9. Pessina, Adriano, *Bioetica – L'uomo Sperimentale* [*Bioethics – The Experimental Man*] Mondadori, 1999, p. 81.

10. Western philosophy defines two main categories of moral theories, distinguishing according to the principle on which they are based: teleological doctrines (from the Greek τέλος + λόγος = purpose + thought) consider actions just based on their effects, while deontological consequences focus on intrinsic properties. In Kant the deontological moral has found its maximum expression, and, in particular, that of "principles" or "intentions," for which the moral evaluation must completely neglect the effects of the action, focusing exclusively on the motives that animate the agent (see Kant, Immanuel, *Foundation of the Metaphysics of Costumes*). To the Kantian perspective, Max Weber added/contrasted the ethics of "responsibility," introducing rationality concerning the aim pursued as a parameter for evaluating moral (see Weber, Max, *Politics as a Profession*).

11. I do not intend to use here the expression "analogical moral" in the sense in which it was used by Habermas, that is regarding the relationship between humans and nonhumans, to be based on analogy as the other would be an alter ego of the agent. In his theory, Habermas refers to the principle of analogy, hence, by extension, the definition of "analogic" of his moral (see Habermas, Jürgen, The Challenge of Ecological Ethics to the Anthropocentric Conception, in S. Della Valle, edited by, *For an Ecological Action*, Baldini & Castoldi, Milan, 1998, pp. 388, 389); on the contrary, the meaning of analog as intended by me refers to the analog reproduction technology, which, unlike the digital one, is not based only on the "on" or "off" conditions, but rather records and reproduces all the states intermediate – the nuances – of the original information.

Chapter 5

Thoughts and Actions to Change the World

Philosophy is usually considered useless, especially nowadays during very pragmatic times.

The word "philosophy" itself has come to indicate something abstract and even harmful, a sort of excessive speculation aimed at dissertating about everything and nothing practiced by alienated people, who, probably, do not have real problems to face daily.

The purpose of this work is to provide conceptual tools to reach conscious behaviors: judgment, such as "good" or "bad," is not relevant. What counts is awareness.

There is no subjective right or wrong, only different levels of awareness, hence the different interpretations regarding these concepts.

We are afraid of questioning others' habits or stereotypes that prevent us from recognizing what is consistent with an idea.

Philosophy, understood as the ability to reflect on the meaning of things and oneself, represents the starting point to act consciously and conceive and promote any change.

This is completely different from studying the history of philosophy, which usually happens at the university. Instead, we should develop a specific thought on our own.

You cannot learn to reason freely if you are always entangled in the thoughts of others and limited to expressing a preference between them: vice versa, it is necessary to become actors of thought.

Too often, we are taught what to think rather than how to think, and it is precisely for this reason that we transform ourselves, from the free thinkers that nature has made us, into the mere voters that habit has made us.

We could say that today the time is ripe to change this state of affairs, but this would be an entirely partial assessment and easily subject to denial: let us, therefore, limit ourselves to noting that, ripe as they were, the time certainly calls for a new approach to thinking and acting, therefore a new philosophy in ideas and approach. This is Eusebism, and for this reason, the last part of the work is dedicated to prodromal reflections on constructive behavior.

5.1 THOUGHTS

Nonviolence

Everything and its opposite have been said and written about nonviolence: that it is right, wrong, absolute or limited to specific cases, cowardly, courageous, useless, necessary, utopian, and so on.

Why would it be right to practice nonviolence instead of, for example, opposing violence with violence?

Even natural law could easily lead us to consider ethics a practice defined as the law of the strongest, or, in a variant, the law of the jungle. We could say that natural equilibrium is based on violence.

A karmically oriented and ethical interpretation explains that any violent act causes damage to the agent.

Finally, there is the practical aspect to consider: many, while proclaiming themselves opposed to using force, justify it in self-defense cases. This creates a problem since self-defense, in its final analysis, simply means defending one's interest, but which interest is worthy of protection using force?

At this point, a further question opens up, which can be resolved or at least faced differently by each one: some would kill to protect the property or economic interest, some to defend themselves from nonlethal aggression, and some only in case of potentially lethal aggression. But what is aggression? When can it be defined as potentially lethal, and when not? Are the preparatory acts sufficient to justify the violent reaction? What can be considered preparatory acts? How much violence is justified in reacting to aggression?

Dozens and dozens of further controversial and potentially unsolvable issues could be listed, but the truth is that no matter how hard we try, we are all affected in various ways by hypocrisy and by the persuasion that our interests deserve more protection than those of others. On these assumptions, justifying abstractly violent behavior would mean opening the door to any harassment: this certainly does not help with the law, or in legitimizing wars, or justifying retaliation, preventive attacks, and evident forms of harassment of citizens and other people in the world.

Human history and actuality show that in the interpretative folds of legitimate violence, it is always in any case allowed to adopt behaviors that, far from eradicating injustices, perpetuate them.

We must note that humanity is not yet mature enough to manage the concept of violence because we cannot determine what is worthy of violence and what is not.

Violence causes more violence, even if many would dissent.

Would we ever be mature enough to understand the correct use of violence? If that day comes, we will know, since we will no longer need violence at all.

Violence is not only material: it could be psychological as well, such as coercion.

Coercion, being a form of violence, must be condemned, and it cannot lead to good, even if goals are good or just. For example, there are some "Illuminati" who think that they can lead the world to a new order, no matters how: even if their new order was magnificent (and we should disagree), forcing others to comply with it through threats, fear and fraud could not be good.

The difference between a forced and a consciously matured behavior is that the first is ephemeral and will determine a similar and commensurate reaction, while the second will be lasting and free of retaliation.

There is no "right" violence: the only just violence is that which is never exercised against anyone.

There is no self to protect at the expense of the other. While it is certainly correct to say that—from a legal perspective—those who merely defend themselves from others' aggression cannot be considered guilty, it is also true that, from a strictly moral profile, to define the violent reaction as right is no different from justifying the initial aggression itself.

It is not wrong to defend oneself from violence. However, it is also not right to use violence in doing so: this is certainly instinctive and natural, but in a perspective of abandoning selfishness, the simple fact of affirming that self-protection can prevail over the integrity of the other is simply contradictory.

Finally, from the political point of view, no form of violence determines a lasting improvement. At this point, one could ask: how to adopt nonviolence and protect the weak and defenseless?

During World War II, allies had to fight against Hitler: this victory resulted in over 70 million military and civilian casualties, years of devastation during the conflict, and years of violent retaliation and reverse persecution after that.

Some argue that sacrifices are the price paid in the name of a greater good such as freedom; just a few years after the end of that conflict, how was the world? The territories subject to the communist dictatorship did not enjoy any freedom but, on the contrary, were subject to repression, controls, and persecutions even higher than those of the fascist and Nazi dictatorships (in the USSR alone, there were over 60 million deaths). In the United States, ten years after World War II, people of color were still not allowed in the same places as white people because racial laws were still in place.

We can conclude that evil was not defeated but rather transferred.

Today, our freedom, apparently guaranteed by constitutions and laws, is limited by corporations that make rules by changing our minds through media, paying politicians, and such.

Western societies financed or participated, directly or indirectly, through military intervention or economic assistance, logistical, or political support, in conflicts within and outside their geographical borders, to the point of coining definitions such as that of "preemptive attack."

The same set of mind is at the basis of neo-imperialism and the establishment of a dictatorship of the economy as opposed to that of an ideology: the result is a planet on the verge of collapse, overexploitation of resources, the persistence at all levels of the mentality of the strongest with the consequent harassment of the weakest, and the affirmation, as a model of life, of an individualistic and consumerist egoism.

What democracy would allow a few to exploit the resources of all the others for their gain, damaging them irreparably and depriving large parts of the world's population of the possibility of accessing essential resources?

Whenever any form of violence is legitimized, a window opens through which we must be aware that those who come after us can potentially let anything pass.

But the concept of nonviolence in the Eusebist perspective transcends its physical manifestation, affecting that of thought and actions that, while not involving the aggression of others, involve forms of harassment or manipulation.

Nonviolent thinking cannot be considered a mere renunciation of expressions that are harmful to the other but must rather take the form of a 360-degree recognition of respect: do not devise oppressive behavior, do not engage in violent words or other expressions.

Verbally assaulting someone can be even worse than punching them, which is why our philosophy of life should lead us to view it just as vile and harmful to ourselves as it is to those whom we use them against to cause offense or pain.

In short, to think in a nonviolent way means to love or at least respect enough, never to consider imposing oneself on others as a good thing.

Therefore, the nonviolent will refuse to impose a behavior or idea on the other, considering both physical and mental coercion equally deplorable.

Discrimination and Discriminations

At this point, it should be clear that the foremost goal achievable through the Eusebist philosophy consists of eliminating all discrimination and the very concept of discrimination.

One of the criticisms that have been advanced against this thought concerns the impossibility of treating everyone in the same way precisely, but this is not the goal to aim since, on the contrary, it responds to a very superficial and shortsighted definition of respect: the true purpose should be to treat everyone correctly based on the differences that distinguish them.

Refraining from discriminating does not mean agreeing on different opinions, nor does it mean accepting or loving everyone: it is simply a matter of avoiding making an a priori judgment toward what we do not like or what bothers us.

To deny the differences is superficial and misleading. If, for example, I say: "I don't like the color blue," my peers believe that I have expressed a legitimate opinion and a completely legitimate preference.

If I say: "I don't like homosexuals," the result is that I will be accused of "homophobia." This is due to confusion on two main elements: on the one hand, we must distinguish between what we do not like and what we are discriminating against; on the other hand, however, we automatically conclude "contempt = discrimination."

In short, we should remember Rousseau, who used to say, "I disagree with what you say, but I will defend to the death your right to say it."

However, discrimination does not simply mean preferring someone of a different race or sex to another one; it is discrimination every time we choose a friend or family member to fill the role that a stranger could do better, when we use our position to benefit a relative, thus harming other strangers.

Any discrimination is nothing other than a line drawn on the ground, through which to establish a priori who will be able to enjoy certain benefits and who will be excluded from them.

As with the use of violence, discrimination can only be rejected or accepted entirely: if we admit a single kind of violence and discrimination, we potentially admit any. Who should determine to what extent violence or discrimination is allowable or not?

Human beings made any discrimination: between the noble and non-noble, men and women, rich and poor, slaveholders and slaves, white and black, Aryan and non-Aryan, humans and nonhumans.

We practice small discriminations every day: the motorist toward the pedestrian or the cyclist, the fan of a team toward others teams' fans, the follower of religion versus other religions, citizen and residents toward immigrants, and such.

We distinguish ourselves into categories to discriminate better, and in this way, we depersonalize individuals, flattening specificities into a single prerogative. Every time we do that, we are legitimizing and perpetuating the paradigm of discrimination: in this way, we can, for example, classify dogs as pets and pigs as food products.

Often, we were not trained in prejudices, and the discrimination is ignorance or lack of awareness.

These simple examples, which each of us can observe every day, demonstrate how anyone can discriminate based on very personal traits, matured based on their personality, character, experiences, social context, inclinations, and such.

Currently, Western societies concluded that it is not right to discriminate between humans. However, apart from the doubts regarding the effectiveness of this principle, it is clear that this does not mean having renounced the concept of discrimination, but rather continuing to endorse it only toward nonhumans.

One of the longest-standing issues that occupy animal rights philosopher's concerns is the identification of a correct discrimination criterion: such approach is rejected by Eusebism, which, on the other hand, promotes the renunciation to any discriminatory parameter.

It would be paradoxical to oppose discrimination and then formulate a criterion for practicing further ones. To affirm that only dogs or monkeys, or perhaps, as Regan did, mammals that are properly developed beyond one year of age, can be comparable to humans, or, more precisely, become the holder of rights, simply means shifting the line of discrimination but not abolishing it completely.

After all, history teaches us that recognizing more rights is an index of social evolution. But at this point, a question spontaneously arises: why wait for the next generation or the next government or the next society, and with them the shifting of the line of discrimination, instead of taking us forward and immediately recognizing that no line has the right to exist and that, if this will not be, it will always fall back into the default of discrimination.

Many of the criteria we use for our discriminations are completely ephemeral or subject to updating: just think of the science that has not yet decided whether a virus is life or not; therefore, how can we adopt partially unknown parameters to lead our actions?

We must have the courage to recognize the infinite differences between everything that exists; we must have the courage to get out of hypocrisy and admit that not everything different from us can please us; we must have the strength to refrain from discriminating against someone just because they are different or because we do not like them.

We will have understood the true meaning of the word "respect" only when we can look at others for what they are, without placing them in categories and labels, and in any case, renouncing to exercise any form of prevarication against them.

So, we can conclude that we must first acknowledge that the differences exist and try not to flatten them as an excuse to reject discrimination. The question we must ask ourselves is: "What difference can justify discrimination?"; the answer: "None."

Denying differences as a premise to respect somebody or something else proves that we do not respect any at all.

Of course, the veto against discrimination does not only concern what we do to others, but also what we demand from them: it is easy to be against discrimination when we are in the group of the discriminated against, but the real challenge is to give it up even when it would be to our benefit.

Using any advantage, for example, in the case of nepotism because of our kinship with a powerful person, implies having harmed someone else who will not access it.

In short, we should learn to relate to ourselves and others based on specificities and without a priori, avoiding those mental categories that accentuate differences, perhaps even creating them where they do not exist, while also bringing legitimacy to them to discriminate.

Evolution and Revolution

Saint Simon used to distinguish between organic and critical epochs: during the former, humanity would be united by a collective and shared purpose, while in the second case, the common bases and individuals would disappear. They would act more on instances that do not qualify as a collective.

After all, what is a society? Why can we use the term "they" instead of "us," speaking—for example—of the ancient Romans? For what reason, when we go through the postwar period, do we identify that society as "ours"?

The forms of government make the difference: the collapse of the Roman Empire, for example, caused the handover from one political system to another: a society died, another was born.

Will whoever comes after us consider himself "other" from who we are today and speak of us as an ancient society? If, one day, United States split, in North America, a new society would rise, and they would call "old USA" that country, feeling it different from theirs.

But borders are not just lines drawn on a map: culture and mental horizons are closely connected with the sense of belonging to a society, so it is not entirely wrong to even refer to historical periods based on different systems at different levels in the common evolutionary path.

Social aspirations are closely connected with the political order: if, for example, 200 years ago there was a struggle to achieve the unity of Italy, today there would be those who have the opposite objective of returning to a division of the national territory.

Why do people keep changing their government forms, borders, and social systems? Probably, the ideal solution has not yet been found. Nevertheless, I believe that the historical, social, and political path we have taken so far demonstrates the wrongness of our approach: for this reason, we still face an alternate of critical and organic epochs.

Unless you think you have reached the perfect political and social form, that therefore our society is definitive, we are just another of the many steps placed on a ladder whose end we still cannot see, nor where it leads.

But if this system based on the continuous reversal or distortion of the preexisting systems has led to so many uncertainties, steps in one direction, and second thoughts or situations even more critical than those we intended to overcome, it is clear that it is not a correct system.

The first mistake in revolutions is that they are antithetical to the considered wrong model: it is not a new independent paradigm but rather a sort of rebellion against something else. But how can a model born as an antithesis to something else failing to be perfect? What are the chances that this new system represents the best from all points of view if substantially its construction is based only on one point of view? Furthermore, addressing something means conceptually adhering to the modalities on which it was based: if, for example, a revolution is carried out to replace one form of government with another, one is implicitly endorsing the principle of centrality and fundamentality of the government itself. One thing is to say: "I want a different government," and another is to say: "I don't need any government."

The revolutions of history have never determined "eternal" changes, but often not even lasting: just thinking about Europe in the last 300 years, one would lose count of how many forms of government, states, rulers, emperors, and revolutionaries have followed one after another and have quickly risen to power, while faster were passed by history.

Of course, one does not revolutionize only a government, but also the thought. A government or an ideology can be imposed by force, but only as long as the force is applied, practiced, or threatened.

Not all revolutions are the same: some, in the face of a similar name, conceal profound ontological differences, which inevitably lead to different outcomes.

Take the Russian communist revolution and the so-called feminist revolution for example. The former was born as the subversion of a preexisting regime and consequent collective imposition of a different regime, regardless of whether it was socially shared or not; the second, on the contrary, represents a movement aimed at spreading awareness and not at imposing a reversal of roles, but, if anything, the pursuit of a better balance. The difference between the two "motions" is that the first was ephemeral, while the second is in continuous evolution: that desired equilibrium has not yet been reached, but everything seems to show that it points in that direction, while nothing suggests the possibility that in the future the course will be reversed.

One cannot replace one evil with another evil, and in any case, it should be clear, if only for the lessons of history, that any imposition of unshared values represents absolute evil, while the serious risk is in making a mistake when one considers oneself a holder—absolute truth and the right/duty to impose it on others.

For all these reasons, when we think about changing the things we do not like, we should first think about how to change ourselves, while any transformation, internal or external, should be based on the concept of evolution rather than that of revolution.

Evolving means increasing one's own and others' awareness, maximizing the balance of prejudices and discrimination: the conflict rate should represent an essential parameter to understand if one is in one or the other hypothesis: if one is making a revolution or an evolutionary process.

Seeking or provoking conflict, directly or indirectly, through choices that lead to this will never contribute to evolution but, if anything, will lead to the typical imposition of the concept of revolution.

If we choose to take revolutionary paths, we must be prepared for the reactions that will ensue by understanding that everything we do will be ephemeral and that the subsequent transformation is likely to be opposite to ours.

Violent actions, born in antithesis to what they oppose, are wrong instruments that will result in harmful effects.

Whenever we focus only on actions, we are wasting energy on the wrong goal on the tangible manifestations of thought rather than on the thought itself. To forbid people to do something previously allowed or vice versa is not a change but a command.

One of the most frequent problems in many organized movements is clear in their names: antifascism, antiracism, antispeciesism, and such.

First, cataloging and giving labels limit the scope. Anti-"something" can discuss any issues, but they will be considered in the first place as "those anti-. . . ."

There is a second problem with the idea of the "anti": such thought is deeply anchored to its nemesis. Every time you mention one, you will recall the other as well.

The third criticality that emerges from the antagonistic model is perhaps less evident but even more pernicious: we try to emancipate ourselves from something we reject, but we allow it to keep us on a very narrow path: that of antithesis.

Eusebism is inspired by the concept of respect and is not born as an "anti" theory.

Suppose we want to interrupt the cyclicality of history and its revolutions, with the systematic emergence, first of one interest, and now of another. In that case, we must broaden our horizons to embrace the entirety of what exists within an all-encompassing evolutionary process without any barriers, preconceptions, or limits.

Politics and Other Fideisms

The term "politics" comes from the Greek *pòlis*, that is, the city: the first organized community within which, given the number of individuals that compose it, there is a need to delegate decision-making power to a small group of individuals, or of government.

Historically, politics was invented to guarantee the interests of the governed as their direct emanation. But, unfortunately, this could only be true in an ideal world, which ours is not: scrolling through Western history and reviewing the evolution of politics, we see an excursus that in the best cases has seen the affirmation of protagonists, selfishness, and excessive powers; in the worst cases – moreover very frequent up to very recent times if not yet present – assassinations, kidnappings, accusations, deceptions, opportunisms, massacres, betrayal of entire peoples, and so on.

We could describe the relationship between rulers and the ruled as having a parabolic trend within a Cartesian plane: if we place excessive power of the ruler on the ordinate axis and the passage of time on the abscissa axis, the result is that from the moment power is conferred, whoever receives it systematically begins to increase it, detaching himself more and more from the interest of those who conferred it. In the end, having reached the peak, the governed intervene (often in a violent way) to rebel against the excessive power, which then collapses vertically rather than with a parabolic trend. At this point, the changes and transformations that we mentioned above take place, and which can be defined as more enlightened, the more they are widely shared; if, on the contrary, the reforms have the aforementioned revolutionary connotation, excessive power will be immediately overturned.

Politics in contemporary Western democracies fully reflect them: if a society considers economic wealth as a parameter of well-being, it will elect as its representatives individuals who leverage these ideas, and therefore interested in enriching themselves.

In short, when we complain about our politicians, we do nothing but complain about how we are ourselves. Still, because we cannot understand it, or, more simply, to admit it, we concentrate our critical capacities on others. So it happens that we cheat in exams and competitions, try to obtain positions through friendships and kinships, strive to accumulate money and other material objects, have power over others, and exploit it for our benefit and for those we care about, but not to do good for others. However, when someone who represents us does so in all respects, acting as we do, we say that we are dissatisfied, amazed, and disheartened.

We cannot have rulers who tell the truth if we do not want to hear it, nor disinterested politicians if we are not, nor selfless people if our cultural model supports selfishness at all levels.

On closer inspection, the problem is not that there are no honest, altruistic, nonmaterialistic, and disinterested people at all: the real problem is that they have to be considered extraordinary in a dishonest, selfish, materialistic society.

If we possessed the values that we would like to see in our politicians every day, we wouldn't even need any government, or laws, nor sanctions to apply them: we would be aware.

A mature and evolved society, completely aware, would not need politics at all. There would be no selfish interests pursued to the detriment of others, nor the need to represent them through opposing political alignments. If anything, there would be a government in charge of ordering and managing what must be ordered and managed.

Politics in our historical context represents the umpteenth excuse to create distinctions, accentuate differences and conflicts, and this always without considering the personal nature of the individuals who make up that system, and who, as mentioned, are simply the translation of values and principles (or their absence) in a society which elects them.

In this sense, politics is just like faith, since expecting our rulers to be better than we are ourselves and believing that they can solve the problems that afflict us represents a utopia and a mere illusion, not unlike that which leads us to believe something irrational, unproven, and very unlikely if not impossible.

Most of the problems we ask politicians to solve are created (or even imagined) by us, that is, by the sum of the individuals that make up a society: who, therefore, has the power to change things? Us or someone else?

5.2 ACTIONS

To be means to act: many people prefer to think that problems afflicting them depend on and can be fixed by others. However, waiting for someone else to do what we are not willing to do ourselves means becoming spectators of life and therefore devoid of meaning.

Refraining from acting is an action in the moral sense of the term: for example, renouncing to participate in an act that is not shared is certainly not inertia due to a lack of activation, but rather the result of reflection.

A fundamental premise of our actions consists in understanding their effective extent, which means not overestimating them, but, above all, not underestimating them either: we must always keep in mind the concept of action and reaction, as well as the domino effect (or, to use a popular modern definition these days, "the viral effect"). Unless we live isolated inside a cave, we continually meet other people who will be influenced not only by the thoughts we communicate to them, but also by our actions. This can alternatively be a source of inspiration or blame.

Although in daily action we tend to make selfishness and, above all, hypocrisy prevail, in truth, we are perfectly capable of understanding when we are doing something aimed only at ourselves and when instead we act disinterestedly.

In a general and abstract way, the first and perhaps. The only principle necessary would be precisely that of considering the expectations of others and supporting them similarly to ours, or, at least, not always considering ourselves superordinate to others; on a more concrete and factual level, especially considering the daily human and social condition, it is worth reflecting on the extreme importance of some choices.

Below we will examine more specifically those preparatory actions for the transformations proposed by Eusebism that each of us can carry out, without the need for captains, instructors, masters, gurus, or simple auxiliaries: in short, we can do it ourselves; conversely, what depends on others will always be limited to the extent to which it finds our approval and application.

Being Informed and Informing

How free are we? Never as today has information played an essential role in the freedom of individuals: the greater the complexity of social specialization, the greater the detachment of the individual from the effects of his decisions.

Let us take a simple example: I decide to buy a product with the promise that it will help benefit some homeless children, as I care about the well-being of all children. The item I purchase is a seemingly harmless textile product. One week after my purchase, a television news report reveals that the textile manufacturer uses children in the third world to make what I have bought: at this point, it can be safely argued that the exploitation canceled out the donation, and that, therefore, the final moral balance is zero. After another month from the first television service, a second investigation discloses that the producer never even donated any of the commercial proceeds to charity: at this point; it becomes clear that my action – buying the textile product – not only financed child exploitation, but did not even achieve any of the beneficial intentions that I had intended.

Most of our decisions are based on opinions that we have not matured after comparative analyses of facts and information, but we live and limit ourselves to accept simple habits rooted in a society without criticism. The more information and choices available to us, the more pressing the need for correct information becomes, at least concerning those fundamental choices that characterize our life.

The alienation of the average individual from food production has reached such levels that it is practically impossible to trace the origins of what is found in an ordinary supermarket. Most people completely ignore even the methods used to make what they consume daily.

Tolstoy used to say that if slaughterhouses had glass walls, we would all be vegetarians: how many of us, during our lives, visit animal farms? Tolstoy's aunt's case helps us to reflect on real freedom of choice. Tolstoy once invited his aunt for lunch, and he was told that she would have required meat. So, the writer had a live hen and a knife put on the table, inviting her to get herself the food she wanted.

How many of us, if put in front of a living animal, with its gaze and perhaps even the unconscious affection that would be able to recognize us (i.e., to recognize who is about to kill it), its unequivocal will to live and it's a sentient being, would be able to hold the knife and not just kill it, but also slaughter it and then cook it?

Who, living in those nations that have now become the dump of the West amid plastic, chemical, toxic waste, pollution, disease, could consider more important the right to change a cell phone a year than the right to survive?

A well-known saying reads "blissful ignorance," meaning that those who live in ignorance are more serene than those who know better the reality in which they live.

At this point, there is a distinction between real and "convenient" ignorance: while in the first case, we are really in good faith in our convictions but simply lack information (that we probably lack), in the second case, we are aware of the truth, but we prefer to convince ourselves that we are not. Thus, for example, some are convinced that global warming does not exist, so they can continue undeterred in their habits, or those who have heard something but prefer not to deepen their understanding of it, simply thinking that they would have to otherwise deal with their conscience.

It might look like a paradox, but we are very exposed to disinformation in the information society.

The first question we should ask ourselves is whether we are the ones who reach the information or the information that reaches us? In the second case, we should automatically ask ourselves who and why they are interested in informing us: a preliminary filter is necessary to purify the news a priori and make predictions about their reliability and usefulness.

Surely advertising messages, which more and more often aspire to bestow real sources of knowledge, cannot be considered disinterested; yet many people almost subconsciously receive notions through commercials, then making them their own.

Today advertising looks more like push or induction: advertisers' purpose is no longer to inform that a product exists or to show its characteristics, but to create a new need. In the viewer, it is persuading him of the usefulness of something that is mostly useless and often even harmful.

Information, especially in advertising, is never absolute since it communicates something but inevitably leaves other things out.

The problem is not only what we know, but, above all, what we do not know: what we did not consider important to investigate, what is deliberately silenced, or simply everything we do not encounter.

Knowledge makes you free: with this awareness, we must act daily to reach information as seekers of truth and not as mere spectators of what others have decided to communicate to us.

The main issue of information conveyed through mainstream (primarily television and press) is that what is said is just what can be said. What can we do? There is no practical use in daily life to know that a guy we have never met has killed his wife in cold blood and will spend the rest of his days in prison. This is of no use to us, and it is precisely for this reason that there is no hesitation in informing us. Quite different is the case of what we can do concretely every day, but that we tend not to want to hear because it would force us to question ourselves, while those who manage the information cannot divulge it. After all, otherwise, they would question the very system to which they belong.

Hence, we can say *recycle* but not *do not consume*: the first represents a way to feed the system, but it is not a solution; the second call offers a solution but questions the system.

One of the main achievements of the internet is precisely the possibility of finding information of all kinds, but, above all, of becoming active protagonists rather than passive spectators.

Getting informed does not mean being sponges who collect everything, but critical researchers who not only find and select news but, above all, put it to good use and act accordingly.

A truly critical researcher renounces prejudice and does not seek simply to confirm what he thinks he knows but is aware that he embarks on a journey of which only the starting point is known. Are we ready to do whatever it takes to find the truth, or do we just want to feel comfortable with our routines?

Information cannot be the vicious circle that we see today; rather, it must become a virtuous circle in which everyone gives and receives. Therefore, the first and highest honor we can aspire to is to provide others with information useful to make them free and aware: we should devote as much time to dissemination as we do toward research.

Informing is also a life practice to be opposed to imposition, whether more or less violent, of thought: the difference between the two modes of action is that while the first puts the individual in his decision-making autonomy (free will) at the center of the evolutionary path, the second is based on a presumption of superiority of an individual on the other, and therefore the need for the first to prevail over the second.

The evolutionary process can never be an induced hetero phenomenon but can only occur spontaneously; otherwise, there is no evolution: if there is an obligation, there can be no choice, therefore not even awareness, which is at the base.

If we want to promote radical and lasting change but, first of all, empower everyone, we must be clear that the difference cannot only be in the ends.

Bottom line: we should get informed and inform others, to become (ourselves) and make (oth free and aware.

Being Free from Addictions

We usually define addictions as physiological or psychological: often, we think about drugs, alcoholics, gambling, and such.

Yet in everyday life, we do nothing but pursue a life model based mainly on maintaining a *status quo*: we cannot renounce some foods, or eating too much, or technological gadgets that are often completely useless or harmful, and so on.

What worries us the most are the changes: to question or modify something we are used to doing in a certain way; it does not matter whether it is destructive to us or others since the habit of doing so prevails overall. As a result, some commit suicide rather than change their lifestyle; some decide to pass over others at any cost, some who are so accustomed to everyday life that they consider it a real value, if not the only one.

In the film *The Matrix*, the character named Cypher represents the contemporary average Western man: instead of accepting reality, with all its problems and limitations, he prefers to flee from it even at the cost of betraying his friends to live in an illusion that guarantees the satisfaction of his senses.

Anyone who ever volunteered knows that you cannot present shocking images or dramatic situations, as people would just move away.

If you have a very bad neighbor, who throws garbage on the street and does recycle, and you call the police, finally forcing him to change his behavior, you will feel good. You could feel like as you have saved the environment. But what if I tell you that you are the problem? Probably, you buy disposable goods, smartphones, and electric cars with heavily impacting batteries, eat animals, favor your friends and relatives over strangers, etc.

How do you distinguish an addiction? Anything unnecessary that we consider a need and that we cannot give up. How to determine what is necessary and what is not? Our answer is usually very “flexible”: we are not ready to admit that we have an addiction, so we prefer to abuse the definition of "necessity," attributing it to the most disparate things.

They say: *if you can't beat them, join them.* It is easier for us to turn addiction into a necessity—thus absolving ourselves—rather than questioning ourselves.

First, we need to overcome hypocrisy: there cannot exist as many needs as there are in our inalienable habits, and therefore we should be able to distinguish what is and what, instead, ourselves or others have convinced us to be.

Can we live free of any additions? Probably, many Western citizens cannot.

A very useful exercise to develop your emancipation from false needs is getting used to changing habits for no reason (besides checking your level of dependence).

So why is it so important to break free from addictions? The answer is simple: to be free. It is not a question of freedom as an end but of the unfailing prerequisite for gaining awareness of ourselves and others and making us promoters of a virtuous circle instead of the vicious one that feeds on addiction.

From the smallest ancient community to the largest industrial civilization, the effect of addictions is visible: whether it is to steal something from someone else, to pollute excessively, to kill, to exploit, to overwhelm, or to manipulate, at the basis of all this. It is easy to find addictions to habits, desires, people, or objects.

Being addicted to something also tarnishes our moral judgments, so that we end up justifying something even when we are perfectly aware that it is—or at least that we believe it—wrong.

Emancipation, or detachment, allows us to identify with greater impartiality the road that leads to the effective balancing of the interests of several subjects, without ours being the superordinate one by definition.

It is not certain that we can free ourselves from addictions. Still, it is harmful to convince ourselves and others that something is right just because we want to continue doing it without feeling guilty.

Most of us do not want to be free or aware: we just do not want to feel guilty.

Helping Others as Yourself

The inspiring principle of many Western countries, solidarity, is affirmed by transversal political parties, religions, and philosophical theories.

Most of the time we talk about solidarity, it is instrumental: for politicians to be elected, companies are considered good people for associations to raise money.

Real solidarity comes from compassion, feelings, and altruism.

What we can do as individuals is what makes the difference: when we follow our feelings, we are right; when others use our feelings, it is wrong.

We need to connect the mind with the heart to avoid manipulations.

The best way to start is by renouncing discrimination and help those who need it, not whom we like or who can help us in return.

The day we will recognize ourselves in others, we will enjoy their satisfaction as a mutual fulfillment. However, we need to protect ourselves against others because we fight against others.

What actions, then, to take to make today a better time?

Small things: good words to those around us, sufficient empathy to understand their sufferings and discomforts, not always expecting to be the first in queues or on the road, helping selflessly, not worrying only about those problems that may concern us and ours conjoined, always considering others as ends and never as means, and such.

No political or religious commandment is needed to understand the logic of all the above or explain what everyone knows well: altruism is a goal to aspire to and selfishness a defect to be deprecated.

One of the main limitations faced by philosophers of solidarity, or more generally those who profess the need to build a society on collaboration and altruism but who reject transcendental theories, is that they do not apply the implications of the theory to themselves. For example, religions usually affirm that you must respect others as yourself; conversely, a layperson claims the right to freely and completely dispose of himself while agreeing on the absolute duty of respect toward others. If the first position is unfounded, since it is based on faith, the second is no less: to affirm that since we are all equal, we are bound to respect others implies that the duty toward ourselves is like that toward those who are different from us. If this were not so, a self-destructive person would be just as entitled to harm others like himself, but if we are unwilling to admit this obvious contradiction, we cannot even conclude that it is morally right to protect others and not oneself.

At this point, it should be clear that the phrase "*you shall love your neighbor as yourself'f* must be interpreted with a double meaning, that is, as a moral duty toward oneself and others.

Those who dispute the self/other equivalence on their own tend to do so for selfish reasons: either because they prefer to override others or to continue indulging in self-destructive behaviors.

If we are all "the same," then the mere fact that we can destroy or damage ourselves does not mean that it is right (or neutral) selves.

Also, the principles of equilibrium and circularity lead us to conclude that no harmful action is aimed at anyone, which remains limited to that individual.

Our availability of ourselves is not unlimited or devoid of moral implications: even altruistic gestures and sacrifices must be tempered within the principle of equilibrium.

Many of us think that sacrifice for someone else or a principle can represent a moral value or even something desirable and deserving: so, we give a more or less literal interpretation of the principle of helping the other *as* oneself.

The principle that requires us to treat others as our equals, however trivially implied this might seem, implies that we are not superior, but also that we are not inferior either: to renounce any individual achievement, or to frustrate, demean, mortify—as, for example, medieval Christianity was led to do—it can never be considered a moral value.

In short, we must not consider ourselves entitled to act against ourselves, even harshly, at our own will: if anything, we should raise the standard of treatment of others as ours to a higher level based on the equilibrium principle.

What could we do to ourselves? The parameter of evolution as the ultimate goal can help: benefiting us or others through material goods is certainly not a step toward evolution, just as it is not giving vent or satisfaction to selfish ambitions.

Small daily gestures make the difference precisely because most of our lives are made up of a succession of these, much more than single exceptional acts. Listening to people, sharing our experiences with them, striving to understand their feelings and needs, taking time for ourselves and evaluating our behavior, satisfying ourselves with the successes and joys of others: doing all this, out of conviction and without expectations of return or rewards, here or there, would be enough to guarantee us heaven on earth.

(not) Consuming

We live in a particular historical period defined as a "consumer society": our lives are entirely organized around economic profit, largely deriving from the production and sale of objects.

This current condition naturally derives from the advent of machines, therefore from the industrial revolution: before then, objects could only be created manually; therefore, we had what we needed, and we paid for quality, not quantity. For logistical reasons, it would have been impossible to increase sales exponentially, as this would have meant increasing the number of workers at the same pace. In artisanal production, everyone achieves what he is capable of, and this in proportion to those who dedicate themselves to the same work. Although optimized and sped up, the craftsmanship requires production rates with relatively narrow, if not entirely marginal, margins. If a tailor takes a day to make a dress and receives ten orders, he will take ten days to make as many clothes as possible: he can remedy this by hiring nine more tailors, thus making ten dresses a day. In a system of this type, the qualitative aspect prevails over the quantitative one, since the tailor himself could hardly think of getting too rich for the simple fact that his customers decide to buy a new suit every day: the simple generational change and the natural wear and tear of clothing would represent good sources of work concerning production potential.

When the machines do men's work, it is possible to determine the exponential production increase mentioned above: at this point, a textile entrepreneur would have a machine capable of producing 1,000 clothes per day and perhaps living in a community of 100,000 inhabitants. In this case, in just 100 days, each citizen could get clothes, and the business could stop. To keep the business alive, the entrepreneur could create the target market itself: if clothes last one year, you could sell no more than 100,000 a year, but if they last half, you could automatically double profits. That is not enough: although people only use one suit at a time, you could convince them of the usefulness of owning more than one suit, perhaps with different shapes and designs. In this way, each of those 100,000 inhabitants would have become potential buyers of at least three, four, five, or more items each year; profits would have skyrocketed.

At first, you satisfy a need; then, you create a (false) need: this is marketing. Or, we could call it a "scam."

Mass production is based on the assumption of the continuous increase in consumption: for this reason, producers need to instigate the market constantly.

In the 1920s, the common incandescent bulbs had reached a remarkable life span, more than 2,500 hours: this posed a serious problem since, lasting so long, it was not necessary to replace them, and manufacturers' profits were dropping. For this reason, in 1924, manufacturers got together. They founded the so-called *Phoebus*[1] cartel. The principle was very simple: to shorten the life expectancy of products to avoid harmful consequences of technological progress and competition. If acting individually, each manufacturer would have tried to maximize the life span of its bulbs to sell more than its competitors; by creating a joint project to reduce that life expectancy, it would have been possible to maintain or increase the sales for everyone without investing in research.

Therefore, the cartel determined that all manufacturers would have to adapt their bulbs to a maximum of 1,000 hours; those found guilty for making longer-lasting bulbs would have been sanctioned based on the deviation from that value.[2]

There is also obsolescence planned[3] to create the market not by forcing buyers to replace defective products, but by inducing consumers to desire new models.

In the digital era, this is called "performance" obsolescence, that is, the need for superior performance to guarantee the functionality of the systems. This method is very fruitful in smartphones, thanks to the continuous updating of operating systems and applications. Currently, the main operating systems for computers and mobile phones are attributable to only three manufacturers: it is extremely easy for them, by systematically increasing the demand for resources, to determine the obsolescence of the devices.

The increase in the use of mobile terminals equipped with batteries has made it possible to limit the phone's life span, thanks to the batteries. While, until 2010, batteries were removable and replaceable, now they are embodied and glued in smartphones. Once, it was possible to replace the battery by buying another one, perhaps not the original brand, but today you need to change the entire item.

Although many think that electric stuff is eco-friendly, it is not: hi-tech waste is the worst, and the same people who claim to be ecological make the worst items in the worst way possible, to make reparations or updates impossible.

On the one hand, we have a few increasingly wealthy producers; on the other many consumers increasingly committed to ensuring constant income to cope with equally constant needs for replacement or updating of products, and, finally, an increasingly important bill to pay.

The dark side of industrial production must be kept hidden as much as possible: factories are outside the cities, often even thousands of miles from the countries where the main consumers reside, who in this way do not see the immense factories and tall chimneys, with their many slaves, less and less human and more and more mechanical.

We must not see children sewing soccer balls, families exterminated by pollution, lands invaded by chemical waste, animals that become extinct alongside the places that allowed their birth and survival.

Nor do we want to see the garbage island off the Pacific Ocean, the radioactive dumps, African children digging into mountains of waste, the birds dying with stomachs full of bottle tops, or fish agonizing in can fittings, and such.

Stopping consumption slows down the economy: so, they say, stigmatizing it.

At the same time, many are forced into a real dependence on mostly unrewarding and alienating jobs, making them servants of consumerism.

It is normal that those few, interested in increasing their profits through the masses, try to feed the system based on the economy, but what is incredible is as their servants of consumerism, rather than seeing in the decline of the economic system a tool of liberation, they persistently continue to want to avoid its collapse, thus fueling the vicious circle.

In short, some (few) subjects have the will to subjugate all the others for their ends, while the latter gives them the chains with which to be bound and directed.

It is simply impossible to expect that someone other than us can change this system: in this role play, those who care only about their wealth cannot, by definition, take into consideration the interests of others, much less place them before their own; only those to be protected, that is us, can make the daily decisions necessary to break the vicious circle.

There is nothing like "ecological" industrial products: anything made on a large scale, even if produced using exclusively "natural" raw materials, still implies exploitation that, for simple quantitative reasons, means it cannot have anything ecological about it.

Any object packed, wrapped, packaged, or transported will necessarily cause waste.

Unfortunately, industrial production cannot renounce consumerism with its numbers, infrastructures, costs, and investments. For this reason, no consumption can be defined as ethical in a contemporary Western society.

We have to rethink from roots our relation with the Earth and our real needs.

We live in a world where bacteria, natural inhabitants of the planet, and promoters of life, are frightening, while we feel reassurance in front of an artificial computer screen: we want an aseptic world in which everything is controlled and ordered according to the will of rulers and corporations. We want large, beautiful, and seedless fruits, "tidy," "clean" and shining houses, bright and perfect clothes, clean, new, and faster transportation, houses that are very warm in winter and very cold in summer, pills to take away any evil, from headaches to sadness.

We do not want to be told that there can be no social justice or respect for people, animals, or the environment, without changing ourselves and our needs: we cannot focus our thoughts and distinguish what we need from what we were convinced to consider a need.

Everything looks easy because we are not involved in it, nor its consequences: we think that "electric" means "green," while it generates tons of toxic wastes around the world, everywhere but in front of us.

We do not want nature: we just want nice, well-ordered yards, where the plants are allowed to live and grow the way we want. They are not ends but mere means.

We use soaps, detergents, deodorants, and antibacterial because they have taught us that nature is dirty, therefore bad: for us throwing the peel of fruit in a lawn is not the natural act to complete a virtuous circle, but an act of vandalism, capable of undermining the foundations of social and civil coexistence.

Everything, even nature with which we surround ourselves, becomes a consumer good: we put and remove plants as we want, and we manage them as machines that must be in the spaces and in the ways for which they "serve," but when they are no longer needed, they become disposable.

Therefore, our vital needs are no longer an unpolluted environment, healthy food, satisfying social relationships, and time to devote to ourselves and our loved ones. Still, artificial places (houses), sterilized even by bacterial life but considered healthy because they are full of synthetic substances, vehicles more for ostentation than for transport, money with which to measure our achievement in comparison to others, and omnipresent and prevalent work over everything else are used to give our loved ones and us a "better" future.

In this consumerist drift, we do not care if our children will be alienated consumers whose main purpose in life will be to work for its entire duration to enrich others.

We do not want that our children become aware or free: we will teach them to kill insects, bacteria, to eat animals, to get smartphones, to avoid other people, and that they are good people because they recycle and drive electric cars.

Every time we decide what and where to buy something, we should ask ourselves:

- Do I need it?
- Do I already have another item that can perform the same function?
- Do I know someone who can lend me that item?
- Is there a similar item with a lower impact?
- Can I buy an item that will last longer?
- Can I buy that object in a more ethical place?

If what we are about to procure has passed the previous scrutiny, it is probably necessary. Otherwise, we must/can refrain from buying, or turn elsewhere, in any case bearing in mind that the only sustainable consumption is the one that is not made.

Feeding Respect

Eating is the most relevant activity for human beings, and making food is the first cause of impact on the environment.

Throughout history, eating habits have changed several times. However, the latest changes in Western countries are based on consumerism: this was not an improvement in nutrition or management of resources, but the opposite.

Marketing also prevailed in the food market, where false needs were created artificially to push consumers to eat and drink more and bad.

Today we have fruits bigger and more beautiful than they once were, seedless oranges, transgenic plants able to survive climatic adversities or so-called parasites, precooked dishes of many types, drinks of every color and flavor, transgenic chickens, cows with antibiotics and hormones, supplements for any need, meal replacements, diet foods, etc.

For the first time in human history, at least on that large scale, food has gone from being a means of sustenance to a source of entertainment. However, this mere sensorial satisfaction is often psychological and aimed at compensating for the daily problems of the consumer society, which wears down human relationships as quickly as the products it feeds on.

Considering that the food supply chain is the human activity with the greatest impact on the planet and its inhabitants, ethics must take into account nutrition.

Unless we feed exclusively on the fruits of our plants, there is no concept of "zero impact" in the food chain in a contemporary society.

Some define vegetable (vegan) food as ethical or "cruelty-free," meaning that it respects the environment and nonhuman animals: it is a trivialization that is certainly not reflected in the reality of the facts. Even if plants do not suffer, or we consider them to be without rights, and therefore consider ourselves devoid of duties toward them, the fact remains that any mass food production cannot ignore the use of invasive and destructive methods that impact the land, insects, and of many animal species. The simple fact that territories are used for cultivation that would have had such vegetation and conformation as the natural habitat of many species implies that we have subtracted them from them by allocating them to our exclusive use. Even if we do not kill animals or exploit them directly, we cannot ignore that taking away their habitat represents the first cause of extinction and a limitation of their rights. We could limit ourselves to "seeing" veganism as the ultimate nutrition goal from a simplified perspective. Everybody said everything about our nature about eating: carnivores, omnivores, herbivores, frugivores, and such.

A little logic would help: until we invented tools for hunting and slaughtering, we certainly would not have been able to eat meat in a meaningful way, much less as long as we were without fire. Likewise, without the ability to cook them, we would not even have been able to eat most of the vegetables we know today. In particular, before introducing farming and agriculture, there was no way to systematically procure those elements that we now consider essential in nutrition: from wheat to milk, from eggs to flour, and such.

Then some argue that hand in hand with the change in diet, our organism would have adapted accordingly: beyond the scientific considerations, there is evidence that anyone can easily ascertain, in particular the fact that even today, the only food that causes us exclusively benefits and of which even the most dedicated nutritionists to meat consumption recommend the intake as necessary and fundamental continues to be fruit. In short, they tell us that we need meat because of proteins and iron, but then they recommend that we should not eat it more than three times a week; on the other hand, they tell us to eat at least 500 g of fruit per day. It would be very curious to conclude that our organisms are designed or adapted to the predominant food consumption of animal origin by listening to such warnings. There is, moreover, a very simple reason why we never hear about tumors, dementia, and diseases resulting from the consumption of fruit: this has always been and continues to be elective food for our species.

The fruit is born specifically to be eaten, unlike any other vegetable or animal: this does not cause the death of the plant, which, on the contrary, uses the fruit precisely for reproduction. This means that eating fruit does not even involve killing a single plant, transforming the environment, producing waste, or changing destinations for other entities.

Some argue that the production of fruit today is not based on the above criteria, and that, for example, fruit plants are eradicated at the end of the season or the end of the economically more profitable cycles and that, however, transgenic plants or pesticides or other industrial cultivation and treatment systems that have a decisive impact on the environment and animals that are used. It is true, but we can say the same about other foods: the difference is that fruit is the most basic food, while other foods are based on fruits and plants. If there is pollution in fruit or vegetables, what about animals fed on these products and sophisticated in their turn?

On the other hand, the current fruit production system must also be modified, both with a view to a return to more nutritious and less "beautiful" products and in respect of the fruit plants themselves; the return to the exclusive consumption of this food can only benefit the transformation process, requiring the adaptation of supply to demand.

We can say that self-respect and respect for others and the environment start from eating.

Omnivorous nutrition cannot be advocated. It is based on the infliction of pain and death on sentient beings, unsustainable for the planet, and determining the economic and social inequality even toward human beings themselves ultimately is seriously harmful to our health.

Most of the greenhouse gas emissions, up to 51 percent,[4] nowadays are due to livestock bred for food purposes; about 60 billion land animals are killed annually to satisfy our whims, but not before being mistreated, imprisoned, mutilated, subjected to all kinds of stress, drug treatments, genetic selections, hormonal therapies, and such. Thus, for example, chickens are so genetically modified that they cannot even survive a few months compared to those weeks necessary for their complete development in the most economically profitable way: muscle hypertrophy makes their bodies unsuitable for the growth and movement of the skeleton, often even within the short term of their miserable lives.

Vegetarianism, as we mean it today, in many respects is no better than the omnivorous diet: the exploitation of production animals of "derivatives" is not unlike those used for meat, not to mention that everyone's destiny is the same. Those who choose to be vegetarians have already chosen empathy and respect, but they probably lack sufficient information or awareness to understand that the use of foods such as cheeses and eggs are still a whim, superfluous, and just as harmful to animals, humans, and the environment, if not more so than the use of meat. In short, it is simplistic and reductive to think that we are acting well simply because what is literally on the plate is not the fruit of death: it is still the cause of death, as well as the suffering, mistreatment, and imprisonment inflicted on animals which, like machines, are transformed into production objects.

Even from an environmental and ecological perspective, drinking cow's milk is no better than eating a steak; on the contrary, it probably has an even greater impact.

The vegan choice undoubtedly represents a step forward regarding the environment, animals, humans, and oneself. Still, it cannot be considered a point of arrival but only a starting point. Being vegan does not mean not exploiting the environment or animals, nor, automatically, doing well for one's health: if it is true that this choice is made from an ethical point of view above the omnivorous and vegetarian ones, it is still evident that, on the other hand, it is placed below the fruitarian or frugivorous one.

The environmental impact of agriculture, including the felling of forests, the use of pesticides, genetic manipulation, more or less natural fertilizers, and the depletion of the earth's resources resulting from intensive farming, is devastating.

Agricultural desertification[5] is the phenomenon that derives from the total enslavement of the soil to cultivated fields, with the removal of any form of plant life other than specific crops, which, in turn, carried out intensively, deprive the earth of the elements that make it fertile and that are artificially added. This explains why wild plants are extraordinarily richer, from a nutritional perspective, than those cultivated.

In short, comparing veganism with fruitarianism is like comparing the omnivorous diet and the vegan diet: in both cases, those who care about the respect of others, whoever they are, and their health and that of the environment will come to the same conclusions.

NOTES

1. Wyatt C. Wells, *Antitrust and the Formation of the Postwar World*, Columbia University Press, 2003.
2. *Co-operative Review*, volume 25, Co-operative Union Limited, Publication Department, 1951, p. 274.
3. Manzone, Gianni, *Il volto umano del marketing* [*The Human Face of Marketing*], Armando Editore, Rome, 2013, p. 115.
4. World Watch Institute, 2009.
5. Virilio, Paul, *La deriva di un continente* [*The Drift of a Continent*], Mimesis, Milan, 1994.

Conclusion

Is Eusebism useful? This is the first doubt that may arise before or after reading this book. It was also my first doubt while I was inventing and developing it.

The purpose, and therefore the usefulness of Eusebism, is to overcome the particularisms, prejudices, and limitations that have characterized human thought and the main philosophical currents. Whether it succeeds is a question that I refer to the reader.

I was not happy with the results of other philosophies, and I thought that we needed to reconnect with the roots of the discipline: once, philosophers were helping human beings to evolve as persons, while, today, even philosophy seems marketing to me.

Describing a new world means rethinking it from the beginning and setting objectives that do not overcome current limits or contrasts. I meant to formulate guidelines that are not valid only "here and now" or only as long as some of the problems they deal with exist.

Starting from the roots (causes), addressing the limits of the present (effects), we will build a system of thought that, having transcended daily routine, will always offer valid references.

If I had to sum up in just two words the meaning of everything that the culture of respect presupposes and implies, these would be *awareness* and *equilibrium*. Respect springs spontaneously whenever there is awareness, and equilibrium also derives from it: this is valid at any level, in any relationship or conflict.

We have always considered the most contingent problems. But, unfortunately, history has not been kind in giving us the outcome of this approach: today, we can get out of the vicious circle and find a world where everyone is a protagonist rather than a spectator.

According to some critics, Eusebism would be excessively idealistic, even utopian: its purposes—say the detractors—would not be achievable, so much to advise against even suggesting them.

I agree with most of the perspectives that conclude that it is impossible to apply all the final changes contemplated by Eusebism today. Still, it is precisely for this reason that I believe it is essential to continuously and strenuously point them out.

Life has taught me that if you aim to hit fifty, maybe you will make it to thirty. If you have underestimated yourself, you might even hit fifty. But you will never make it to fifty-one.

The purpose of universal thought is to transcend the here and now, open wider horizons, which is 100 (or which can even be beyond 100, that is, beyond than currently feasible), and that moving in that direction still represents an improvement.

Our meaning in the universe and the refinement of who we are as individuals and as a community will not be resolved or completed when, for example, we have achieved rights for minorities, animals, or respect for the environment: for this reason, limiting ourselves to philosophies that deal with single problematic aspects is a bit like reading a book without the end. So what should we do with "everything else" once those individual aspects are settled? The proposal of Eusebism is simple and clear: to adopt universal principles and parameters.

In the next future, we will face changes that we have never figured before: the best way to deal with them is by keeping strong, absolute, and universal principles that can lead us to realize who is trying to help us and who is trying to use us. In the same way, we will be able to realize if we are using others or cooperating with them.

Above all, we should be able to recognize and respect freedom and self-determination because our lives and our choices are based on that: who does not respect freedom does not respect anything.

Bibliography

Anderson, Robert S., Beatty, Richard, *Insects and Spiders of the World*, Marshall Cavendish Corp, 2002.

Asimov, I., Silverberg, R., *Robot NDR-113*, Bompiani, Milan, 1992.

Baker, Joanne, *50 Great Ideas You Really Need to Know*, Quercus, 2010.

Bekoff, Marc, Pierce, Jessica, *Wild Justice: The Moral Lives of Animals*, The University of Chicago Press, 2009.

Bentham, Jeremy, *An Introduction to the Principles of Morals and Legislation*, pp. 282–283 (J. H. Burns & H. L. A. Hart, Athlone Press, 1970).

Bentham, Jeremy, *Rationale of Judicial Evidence*, 1827.

Bertholet, Edouard, *La reincarnazione nel mondo antico* [*Reincarnation in the Ancient World*], Edizioni Mediterranee, 1994.

Bobbio, Norberto, Diritti umani e società [Human Rights and Society], in *Sociologia del diritto* [*Sociology of law*] 1989, n. 1.

Bonnet, Corinne, Scarpi, Paolo, *Religions Orientales – Mystic Cults: Neue Perspektiven – Nouvelles Perspectives – Prospettive nuove*, Verlag, 2006.

Brandt, Richard B., *A Theory of the Good and the Right*, Oxford University Press, 1979.

Calvani, Vittoria, Giardina, Andrea, *Le vie della storia* [*The Streets of History*], vol. 2, Editori Laterza, 1979, 1986.

Charles, Jay Daryl, *The Unformed Conscience of Evangelism: Recovering the Church's Moral Vision*, Intervarsity Press, 2002.

Co-operative Review, vol. 25, Co-operative Union Limited, Publication Department, 1951.

Falcòn Y Tella, J. M., Falcòn Y Tella, F., *Fondamento e scopo della pena: diritto di punire?* [*Basis and Purpose of the Sanction: Right to Punish?*], Giuffrè, Milan, 2008, p. 87,

Fenchel, Tom, *The Origin and Early Evolution of Life*, Oxford University Press, USA, 2003.

Francione, *Animals as Persons: Essays on the Abolition of Animal Exploitation*, Columbia University Press, 2009.

Goldberg, Bruce, *Past Lives, Future Lives*, Armenia Editore, Milan, 1992, p. 183.

Hare, Richard Mervyn, *Pensiero morale* [*Moral Thought*], Il Mulino, Bologna, 1969.

Hawking, Stephen, *Dal Big Bang ai buchi neri – Una breve storia del tempo* [*From the Big Bang to Black Holes – A Short History of Time*], Rizzoli, Milan, 1988.

http://www.eco-action.org/dt/thinking.html (last visit: 06/19/2021).

https://link.springer.com/referenceworkentry/10.1007%2F978-3-642-11274-4_1128

https://www.britannica.com/topic/deep-ecology (last visit: 06/18/2021).

https://www.merriam-webster.com/dictionary/law (last visit: 06/20/2021).

https://www.merriam-webster.com/dictionary/primordial%20soup (last visit: 06/20/2021).

Huxley, Aldous, *Perennial Philosophy*, Harper & Brothers, 1945.

Kant, Immanuel, [1784–5] 1997: 212 [Ak 27: 459].

Kant, Immanuel, *The Metaphysics of Morals*, 1797.

Lanza, Robert, *A new Theory of the Universe*, The American Scholar, 2007.

Lanza, Robert, Berman, Bob, *Biocentrism: How Life and Consciousness are the Keys to Understanding the True Nature of the Universe*, Benbellabooks, Inc, 2009.

Lavoisier, Antoine, *Traité Élémentaire de Chimie*, 1789.

Levi, Arnold Post, *From Homer to Menander: Forces in Greek Poetic Fiction*, volume 23, University of California Press, 1951.

Lovaglia, Michael J., *Knowing People: The Personal Use of Social Psychology*, Rowman & Littlefield, 2006.

Manodori Sagredo, Alberto, *Anfiteatri, circhi e stadi di Roma* [*Amphitheatres, Circuses and Stadiums of Rome*], Newton & Compton, 1982.

Manzone, Gianni, *Il volto umano del marketing* [*The Human Face of Marketing*], Armando Editore, Rome, 2013.

Naess, Arne, *The Shallow and the Deep, Long-Range Ecology Movement: A Summary*, in *The Deep Ecology Movement: An Introductory Anthology*, of Alan Drengson and Yuichi Inoue, Berkeley, North Atlantic Books, 1995.

Pessina, Adriano, *Bioetica – L'uomo Sperimentale*, [*Bioethics – The Experimental Man*] Mondadori, 1999.

Peter, J. Shull, *Non-destructive Evaluation: Theory, Technics, and Application*, CRC Press Book, 2002.

Plato, Teeteto, 166 D = DK80 A 2 1.

Ostrander, Elaine, Ruvinsky, Anatoly, *The Genetics of the Dog*, 2nd ed., CPI Group, UK, 2012.

Rawls, John, *A Theory of Justice*, Oxford, 1971.

Reale, Giovanni, *Invitation to Ancient Thought*, La Scuola Publishing, Brescia, 2011.

Regan, *The Case for Animal Rights*, University of California Press, 1983, p. 243.

Regan, Tom, *Empty Cages – The Challenge of Animal Rights*, Sonda, Casale Monferrato (AL), 2005.

Ryder, R. D., *Victims of Science. The Use of Animals in Research*, London, Davis-Poynter, 1975.

Scquizzato, Paolo, *As a Principle – Reflections on the Book of Genesis*, Effatà Editrice, Turin, 2010.

Serafin, Gianandrea, *L'interpretazione del crimine* [*The Interpretation of Crime*], Tangram, 2012.

Singer, Peter, *Animal Liberation*, 1975, Harper Perennial Modern Classics; Updated ed. (2009).

Singer, Peter, *Practical Ethics*, Cambridge University Press, 4th edition, 2011.

Singh, U., *A History of Ancient and Medieval India: From the Stone Age to the 12th Century*, Prentice Hall, 2009.

Suave, David J., *Effects of Deforestation*, 2013, eBook. Vajpeyi, Dhirendra K., *Deforestation, Environment, and Sustainable Development*, Praeger, 2001.

The arrival of Wang, Manetti Bros., Iris Film, Italy, 2011.

Virilio, Paul, *La deriva di un continente* [*The Drift of a Continent*], Mimesis, Milan, 1994. www.almaobservatory.org (last visit: 06/22/2021).

Wyatt C. Wells, *Antitrust and the Formation of the Postwar World*, Columbia University Press, 2003.

Index

About the Author

Carlo Prisco is a lawyer and PhD in Philosophy of Law, an assistant professor at the State University of Milan in Philosophy of Law and Bioethics, the author of "The Right to Vegetarianism" (Hamilton, 2016), the Italian translator of "Animals as Persons" by professor Gary L. Francione, and the creator and founder of the moral philosophy Eusebism. Carlo Prisco volunteered for years in animal advocacy organizations and, as an attorney, promoted vegan people's rights.

www.ingramcontent.com/pod-product-compliance
Ingram Content Group UK Ltd.
Pitfield, Milton Keynes, MK11 3LW, UK
UKHW020842290926
15470UKWH00004B/1495

9 781666 902921